CONTEMPORARY COMMUNITY HEALTH SERIES

The Deepening Shade

THE
DEEPENING
SHADE

Psychological Aspects
of Life-Threatening Illness

BARBARA M. SOURKES, Ph.D.

University of Pittsburgh Press

Published by the University of Pittsburgh Press, Pittsburgh, Pa. 15260
Copyright © 1982, University of Pittsburgh Press
Feffer and Simons, Inc., London
Manufactured in the United States of America

Library of Congress Cataloging in Publication Data

Sourkes, Barbara M.
    The deepening shade.

    (Contemporary community health series)
    Includes bibliographical references.
        1. Critically ill—Psychology.   2. Terminally ill—Psychology.   3. Cancer—
Psychological aspects.   4. Psychotherapy.   I. Title.   II.   Series.   [DNLM:
1. Neoplasms—Psychology—Popular works.   2. Terminal care—Popular works.
QZ 201 S724d]
R726.8.S62   1982   616   81-16276
ISBN 0-8229-3456-6   AACR2
ISBN 0-8229-5337-4 (pbk.)

The following excerpts are reprinted from *The Collected Poems of Theodore Roethke*
by kind permission of Doubleday & Company, Inc. and Faber and Faber, Ltd.: from
"I'm Here" copyright © 1956 by Theodore Roethke; from "In a Dark Time" copy-
right © 1960, "The Long Waters" copyright © 1961, "Journey to the Interior"
copyright © 1961, and "The Far Field" copyright © 1962 by Beatrice Roethke as
Administratrix of the Estate of Theodore Roethke. Excerpts from "The Mire's My
Home" and "The Plain Speech of a Crow," from *Straw for the Fire* by Theodore
Roethke (1980), are reprinted by permission of the University of Washington Press.
I am grateful to the Josephson family for permission to use the poem "Life is so
strange" by Karen Beth Josephson.

for Margaret

In a dark time, the eye begins to see,
I meet my shadow in the deepening shade.
                              —*Theodore Roethke*

Contents

Acknowledgments

THE INITIAL CONCEPTUALIZATION for this book was done with Lois Silverstein Jaffe in 1976. At that time, and until her death two years later, Ms. Jaffe was an Associate Professor of Social Work at the University of Pittsburgh. She was a gifted individual and a beloved friend, and thus her presence is felt in this book.

Thanks are extended to David Epperson, Dean of the School of Social Work, University of Pittsburgh, for his interest in the proposal. It was he who introduced me to Frederick Hetzel, Director of the University of Pittsburgh Press. My contacts with Mr. Hetzel over these past two years have been extremely valuable. Acknowledgment is also due to Philip Hallen, President of the Maurice Falk Medical Fund, for assistance in preparation of the manuscript.

My colleagues and friends at the Sidney Farber Cancer Institute and the Children's Hospital Medical Center in Boston have encouraged me with their interest and humor. In particular, I wish to express appreciation to Harvey Cohen, Associate Professor of Pediatrics, Harvard Medical School, for the clarification of medical concepts. Margaret O'Malley-Keyes, who typed the manuscript, has been a loyal friend throughout. My heartfelt thanks are extended to the many families who have allowed me the privilege of entering their lives.

Most profound is my gratitude to Margaret Clare Kiely, Associate Professor of Psychology, University of Montreal,

Acknowledgments

for her constant availability and perspective, and in particular, for the concept of "neutral time." It is with deep love that I have dedicated this book to her.

Prologue

LIFE-THREATENING ILLNESS IS AN EXPERIENCE of psychological complexity and intensity. *The Deepening Shade* presents a synthesis of the critical issues which confront the patient, family, and caregiver. Rather than a focus on terminality and death, the impact of living with a life-threatening illness is explored. By establishing a structure of the interwoven themes, individual dynamics and intervention strategies may he integrated.

A life-threatening illness is a disease whose diagnosis portends the possibility of death as a final outcome. In *The Deepening Shade*, cancer is used as the paradigm of a life-threatening illness: death, when it occurs, is often preceded by a prolonged period of living with the illness. While in some instances recovery and even cure may be achieved, the patient and family will nonetheless experience the reverberations of anticipatory grief. The psychological observations of cancer patients described in this book are applicable to individuals with other life-threatening illnesses, whether or not the threat of death is transformed into actuality.

The Deepening Shade addresses a wide audience of professionals and paraprofessionals who work with patients with life-threatening illnesses. The book is intended particularly for mental health professionals: psychologists, psychiatrists, and social workers. Physicians, nurses, and allied health personnel comprise another sector of its readership. Also included are chaplains and volunteers in health care settings.

Prologue

Within the book, patients and families affected by life-threatening illness may find a context for their own experience. *The Deepening Shade* can serve as an integrating medium for the professional, as well as an introduction for students in the various disciplines. Throughout the book, the terms "therapist" and "caregiver" are used. "Therapist" denotes the mental health member of the interdisciplinary team. The ramifications of that specific role may be generalized to the other caregivers.

The opening chapter, "Psychotherapy," establishes the structure for the book. While psychological intervention is the specific subject, its implications are relevant for all health care professions. "Life Cycle Issues" and "Loss" illustrate how individuals, regardless of age, share in a common struggle. The chapters "Diagnosis," "Neutral Time," "Anticipatory Grief," and "Terminal" describe the process of life-threatening illness as it unfolds through time. In the annotated interview, "A Life of My Own," essential themes are articulated. Overall, *The Deepening Shade* provides a holistic perspective on psychological aspects of life-threatening illness.

1

Psychotherapy

I learned not to fear infinity,
The far field, the windy cliffs of forever,
The dying of time in the white light of tomorrow,
The wheel turning away from itself,
The sprawl of the wave,
The on-coming water.

—*Theodore Roethke*

TIME IS A UNIVERSAL PART OF EXPERIENCE. It dictates our orientation to past, present, and future in the totality of any moment. In daily life, we have the luxury of oscillating among the three perspectives: we live in the present, with hope for the future based upon the experience of the past. Our sense of time is internalized so that we take it for granted.

Awareness of the irreversible passage of time pervades any experience of potential or imminent loss. Thus a diagnosis of life-threatening illness acutely heightens the sense of time for the patient and family. Its subjective meaning is inextricably entwined with the reality of the clock and calendar. Time becomes the organizing pivot of the experience: "If one can eliminate time sense, one can also avoid the ultimate separation that time brings—death" (Mann, 1973, p. 6). It is this omnipresent awareness of time that makes the threat of loss more critical than any other life stress.

The diagnosis of a life-threatening illness leads many individuals to enter psychotherapy. Their focus is the emotional stress engendered by the illness, rather than more general intrapsychic and interpersonal concerns. As a six-year-old child explained: "I felt much better because I knew that I had somebody to talk to all the time. Every boy needs a psychologist! To see his feelings!"

Aspects of the psychotherapeutic framework include: time; space; the identity of the patient; the therapeutic content and process; and the therapeutic relationship. How that structure is defined will vary in the exigency of life-threatening illness. This flexibility does not give the therapist license to ignore, reject or take lightly basic ground rules. Rather, the utmost challenge lies in adapting a structure to the impinging reality without sacrificing the uniqueness of the therapeutic interaction.

Time

The time commitment in psychotherapy has three facets: frequency, duration, and appointed time of sessions. In traditional psychotherapy, this structure is critical to the containment of the process. Thus there is both theoretical and practical adherence to the "fifty-minute hour." With illness and approaching death as the reality at hand, the scheduling of sessions may vary considerably. Whereas the traditional structure is optimal for the patient during certain phases, there are times when more fluidity is necessary. Effective availability is based upon this recognition, and implies the therapist's consistent and abiding presence.

FREQUENCY

How does the abstraction of availability translate into specifiable properties regarding time? Not only is there an ebb and flow in the frequency of sessions, but also the patient must be given specific "permission" to participate in the regulation. Within a traditional model, any modification of the framework by a patient may be interpreted as manipulation or resistance. The therapist must certainly be alert for such motivation, whether conscious or unconscious, in the patient with a life-threatening illness. Nonetheless, the basic contract can allow for patient-initiated regulation as a norm; its meaning may be inferred within the therapeutic context.

The patient's request for more frequent contact during a stressful period often parallels the reality of the illness process. Conversely, one encounters phases when patients request diminished frequency, if not cessation, of sessions. The reasons for such a request may be highly adaptive to the individual's functioning. The patient who is facing the enormity of loss may at times need to control his or her emotional thermostat, and shut off confrontation and intensity. In exercising this option, the patient must be secure in the knowledge that contact with the therapist may be reinitiated without fear of reprisal.

The understanding that the frequency of sessions may vary is a sine qua non of psychotherapy with patients with a life-threatening illness. A therapist who responds to the patient's "self-regulation" as a narcissistic blow to the sanctity of the process has not accepted this modification. Expressions of relief at lapses in the process may reflect the therapist's own difficulty in handling intensity on a sustained basis. The patient's retreat may be in reaction to such cues.

The frequency of sessions also depends upon whether the patient is being treated in the hospital or in an outpatient clinic. Time assumes a different meaning in the hospital. Hours and days often stretch out so that more frequent meetings, even on a daily basis, may not feel different to the patient from weekly sessions. During brief or uneventful admissions, there may be no need for such an increase. Whether or not the therapist works at the treatment institution will place bounds on his or her availability. However, telephone contact can bridge. time between sessions or, if necessary, serve as a temporary substitute for face-to-face encounters.

DURATION

The duration of individual sessions depends on the patient's physical status, as well as on the concerns at hand. The therapist's goal for a session may be as simple as providing reassurance of continued presence, or it may be to facilitate the patient's working through of an issue. Meaningful exchange can be accomplished by words, touch, silence. What is critical is that the therapist not lose sight of the agenda in the intensity of the moment.

On occasion, particularly during hospitalizations, the therapist must interpret the meaning of a patient's illness behavior. For example, the patient may claim to be too sick to see or talk at any length with the therapist. Is the patient really incapable of interaction, or is the illness being used as a means of avoidance? An error in interpretation in either direction can be damaging to the therapeutic alliance.

If the therapist implies that the patient is using the illness to avoid emotional issues, when the patient is in fact physically drained, a "blame-the-victim" cycle is set in motion. The patient experiences justifiable resentment at the accusation. At some later point, he or she may confront the therapist. However, it is often too threatening for a patient to express anger toward a caregiver and thus the basic trust of the therapeutic alliance may be ruptured beyond repair. Another avenue is that taken by the patient who passively accepts being labeled an "avoider." The vulnerability and powerlessness in the face of physical illness are now further exacerbated for this individual.

The therapist must maintain caution in another direction: that of permitting a patient to disengage under the guise of the illness when, *in fact*, the patient is clinically depressed. While the patient gives messages of wanting only to be left alone, on a more basic level, he or she may be overwhelmed by depression, yearn for contact, and yet be unable to take the initiative. The firm, persistent, and gentle efforts of the therapist are often a turning point in the patient's reengagement.

What cues are available for the therapist to make a differential interpretation of illness behavior? First, it is imperative that the therapist understand the patient's medical condition. There is no substitute for facts. Second, the therapist weighs the patient's self-report and his or her own observations. Third, and of utmost importance, the therapist must communicate with other members of the caregiving team. They can give a general index of the patient's physical and emotional status, which then serves as a baseline for the therapist's assessment.

APPOINTMENT TIME

The structured and secure expectation of meeting at a regular time can do much for the patient's sense of stability within the therapeutic relationship. During hospitalizations, an appointed time provides the patient with a critical pivot for the day. However, as much as is positive in the regularity, there are obvious drawbacks to the "office-hours" regimen. What happens during evenings, nights and weekends, times for which fears of illness and death hold no respect?

The Deepening Shade

I have mentioned many times what I call the "2 A.M. syndrome."
It is in the middle of the night when I feel the most depressed.
The dark is associated with death; there is the feeling that you are
going to die alone; and there are times when I really feel the need
to talk to somebody. Unless there's an available resident, intern
or nurse, there is nobody to talk with. . . . That's where there is
a real deficit.   (Jaffe, 1978, p. 177)

That night was a bad night. It must have been about two in the
morning when I woke up. The little room was pitch dark. . . .
There came upon me a terrible sense of aloneness, of vulnerability,
of nakedness, of helplessness.   (Alsop, 1973, p. 19)

Of the various means of dealing with the "2 A.M. syndrome," few have been tapped by mental health professionals.
As a general solution, the patient is encouraged to discuss the
night fears during regular therapy sessions. An adolescent
thus commented to his therapist: "I do all right all day. My
aggression comes out at night." As the anxiety is brought to
light, its intensity and frequency of occurrence may diminish.
However, it is common knowledge that the patient may never
mention the night fears during the day, even in response to
the therapist's direct inquiry. Somewhat paradoxically, it is
daylight which provides a cover for the dark.

What emerges is the necessity for a flexible "on-call" schedule among therapists working with these patients. A patient's
fear of being alone and abandoned—at the root of night
anxieties—is often assuaged simply by knowing of the therapist's availability. Furthermore, night staff can be trained in
focused listening skills and thus provide a measure of comfort
and relief.

8

Psychotherapy

Space

Space—the physical setting—establishes concrete boundaries for the therapeutic process. As the therapy hour is a time apart, so the setting affords a private space apart from daily life. The office becomes an extension of the therapist, with some of the same projective attributes.

A woman had a regularly scheduled therapy session prior to each hospital admission. She often verbalized how the therapist's office was a "refuge" before the onslaught. Upon hearing that the therapist would be away at the time of her next admission, the patient asked whether she might sit in the office alone. She felt that just being in the setting would help to prepare her.

With the physically ill patient, a consistent setting cannot always be depended upon for structure. Whereas the therapist's office serves as the base, other locations include the clinic, hospital, or the patient's home. Especially when the patient is seen in the hospital, the setting no longer stands protected and apart. Rather, the therapeutic process is enmeshed in the physical and emotional confrontation of the illness.

A hospital affords little privacy. Thus therapy sessions may be constricted, interrupted, or abbreviated by the presence of other patients, visitors, or staff. Another aspect is the lack of bodily privacy for the hospitalized patient. Nudity, exposure, and scrutiny become part of the expected routine. Patients appreciate the fact that, unlike most caregivers, the therapist is not directly involved in physical care.

The hospitalized patient may at times experience the thera-

9

pist's presence as engulfing because the framework is altered: the therapist comes to the patient. Individuals in therapy, particularly children and adolescents, often use "time out" or leave sessions early to cope with intensity. With curtailment of physical autonomy, the patient's anxiety may escalate dramatically. It is a rare patient who asks directly that the therapist leave or that a session be ended. In compensation for this sense of "captivity," the therapist must be acutely sensitive to the patient's cues concerning spatial boundaries.

In the weeks following his amputation, a ten-year-old child cursed and screamed whenever his caregivers entered the room. His reaction was, in part, a desperate plea for space and distance at a time that he felt trapped, without option of escape. The therapist thus held initial sessions for only a few minutes, increasing their duration gradually with constant reassurance of her return. Such respect for the boy's vulnerability permitted him a sense of control and trust. Within a few days, he could accept the therapist and other caregivers more openly, without a sense of overwhelming threat.

Identity of the Patient

In traditional psychotherapy, the identity of the patient is strictly defined: individual; couple; parent-child or family. Many therapists feel that once the definition is established, it should not be changed. The boundaries of confidentiality are similarly explicit. When a therapist works with the patient with a life-threatening illness, the contract regarding "who is seen" is more open from the start. Although psychotherapy may be initiated with the physically ill patient, or with a family member, this one individual becomes the therapist's point of entry into the family system. By no means does all individual therapy become family-based. However, in the face of life-threatening illness, bridging maneuvers to involve the entire family can be critical.

Individual staff members may also seek out the therapist for help in dealing with their own experience.

A physician requested a private appointment with the therapist, in order to clarify the source of his depression and exhaustion: "How much of my feeling is due to the imminent death of my favorite patient, and how much stems from uncertainties in my personal life?"

A nurse whose mother had recently been diagnosed with an advanced malignancy was having enormous difficulty in facing cancer "on two fronts," work and home. As the outcome of several sessions with the psychologist, she decided to take a leave from the oncology unit.

Geist (1977) points out that the therapist's response to these requests can enhance the working relationship. The staff gain in psychological sophistication and show increased empathy for patients. A deeper bond between the therapist and other team members in turn fosters intimacy in patient care.

Because of this broader definition of the identity of the patient, confidentiality becomes a more complex issue. In a family confronting life-threatening illness, the boundaries of confidentiality may be more permeable than is traditionally dictated. The therapist bears heightened responsibility for handling privileged communication within an emotionally intense system. Skill is required to convey the facts and implications of the therapeutic material, without exposing its essence.

Issues of confidentiality can usually be worked out within the family, if the therapist remains sensitive to their potential loss. Individual are encouraged to share feelings with others in the family, either on their own or as facilitated by the therapist. Maintaining confidentiality can be paricularly complex in dealing with children and adolescents. The child must be secure in the "safety" of the therapeutic relationship, while at the same time understanding the need for contact between the therapist and parents. It is critical that the therapist not become a divisive wedge between parents and child or be viewed with a sense of threat as the bearer of secrets which cannot be shared. Most children express relief at knowing of this communication, provided that their own relationship with the therapist remains intact.

As long as a child's psychotherapy sessions were kept separate, he did not protest the therapist's meetings or telephone contact with his parents. He knew that these discussions focused on his coping with the illness. Interestingly, when his mother was upset one day, the child suggested that she talk to the *other* psychologist in the clinic.

Adolescence is a time when privacy and confidentiality are paramount concerns. This is especially true for the adolescent who feels physically and emotionally exposed by life-threatening illness. For this reason, a team of co-therapists to work with the patient and the parents can be particularly effective. Although there is ongoing communication between the two therapists, the adolescent appreciates the less direct link between his or her own therapist and the parents. The therapist can thus provide a sense of emotional sanctuary for the adolescent.

Psychotherapy

The therapist plays a pivotal role in the integration of the patient's total care. With the ethic of confidentiality as a guide, and with the patient's consent, the therapist may share selective aspects of the therapeutic material with the caregiving team. The therapist communicates only essential content which bears directly on the care of the patient. Included are: a statement of the patient's emotional status, with the precipitating event if relevant; implications for the individual's ability to cope; and recommendations for care by other team members. Information which does not contribute to these categories is generally best left unsaid. The intimate nuance and subtlety of the material belong exclusively within the therapeutic relationship.

A woman with leukemia was exceedingly depressed during a routine hospitalization. The staff did not understand the marked change from her typical outgoing manner. In talking with the therapist, the woman revealed that just prior to admission, she had heard of another patient's relapse. She was frightened by the implications for her own situation. Once the woman's reactive depression was explained, the anxiety of the staff diminished, and they were able to provide her with the extra emotional care she needed.

Rumors abounded as to whether the mother of an adolescent patient had died naturally, or had committed suicide. The girl confided to the therapist that the death had been a suicide, and talked at length about its impact on her. The therapist's communication to the staff included: the fact that the patient's mother had committed suicide after a long psychiatric history; the feelings of abandonment and guilt described by the girl; how the experience might affect her coping with the illness; and her need for reassurance despite a counter-dependent facade. When the therapist provided factual data, the "sensationalism" vanished, and the staff developed particular sensitivity toward this patient.

Therapeutic Content and Process

A hallmark of traditional psychotherapy is the unstructured flow of content and process. Past, present, and future interweave in the unfolding of themes. Letting a process emerge at its own pace and time is a luxury precluded by the very nature of life-threatening illness. Its immediacy demands a focus on the present, framed by the themes of separation and loss.

The patient's and family's previous experiences with loss will bear significantly on the present. Thus, an individual's "loss history" is a critical tool in highlighting areas of strength and vulnerability. The history encompasses loss in its broadest sense; for example, through illness and death, termination of relationships (such as divorce), geographical separation, and loss of employment. The history should include the person's earliest memory of loss from childhood, subsequent experiences up to the present, and a description of how the individual functioned in each context. What were the most stressful aspects of the experience? What type of support was positive, deleterious, or lacking altogether? It is of utmost importance to know the patient's and family's past "acquaintance" with the illness they are now facing. Have they known anyone with the disease, and if so, what was its trajectory and outcome? The meaning of the same diagnosis can vary dramatically depending upon these factors. Through this care-

14

fully focused assessment, the groundwork is laid for therapeutic intervention.

One "loss history" revealed that many family members, including children, had perished in the Holocaust. The diagnosis of advanced disease in an only child and grandchild precipitated a massive depression throughout the family system. The grandmother lamented: "We lost so many already, and now. . . .What more can we bear?"

A man diagnosed with an early-stage malignancy was given an excellent prognosis by his physician. Despite this reassurance, however, the patient maintained that he was sure to die within the year. It turned out that the one person he had known with the same disease had died, and thus he viewed his own diagnosis as an unequivocal death sentence.

Those who work with the individual with a life-threatening illness view psychological defenses as coping mechanisms for the present, rather than as barriers to the past. An individual's defensive structure has developed over a lifetime of negotiating reality. Faced with the ultimate reality—the threat of death—his or her defenses may be mobilized to the hilt. Defensive patterns which appear to be constructive for the patient are identified as "psychological tools." Those with deleterious impact become grist for the therapeutic process of change. The therapist thus serves as an advocate of the patient's defensive structure, in the service of optimal coping.

There is a future thrust for both patient and family, albeit in markedly different ways. The family must focus on plans which go beyond the patient's illness and death. Fear and guilt often accompany the acknowledgment that despite the loss of one family member, life does continue. The patient, on the other hand, can consider the future only within the context of the present illness. In the words of a child with leukemia: "The doctors think my bone marrow is fine for now, and *for now* is *for now*." For the patient, the future is inextricably bound in contingency; for the family, the future means continuity.

> And as my diet and my tumor have restricted my movements in space, so the probability that I shall die soon has restricted me to the immediate present in time. It has erected around me an invisible barrier that I bump into a dozen times a day. . . . I'm reasonably sure I'll be alive a month from now, and I sincerely hope I'll be alive three months from now; but beyond that I don't know. . . . In short, I have no future any more. And that I think is the greatest change of all. (Bell, 1961, p. 46)

The therapist must constantly maintain an acute awareness of both the cognitive and affective facets of time (Sourkes, 1977). On a cognitive level, the therapist monitors the reality of temporal issues; for example, how long the patient is expected to live, when the family is available, how much time should be devoted to therapeutic intervention at different points in the illness. For the patient and family, however, cognitive time may be out of phase with its affective counterpart. Thus, a family may panic over separation when in fact, the patient's condition is stable and death is not imminent. Or in contrast, a denial of impending loss may occur when time is short. These seeming inconsistencies arise from the fact that the patient and family live within a dualistic realm of time. The clock and calendar, by their imposition of finite

16

limits, bespeak the reality of adult-time. Especially in confronting life-threatening illness, "the calendar is the ultimate materialization of separation anxiety" (Bergler and Roheim, 1946, p. 190). In contrast is child-time: the magical, omnipotent belief in endless time forever. While the context for psychotherapy is finite time, a shift into child-time does not necessarily imply denial or blocking.

A man acknowledged that there were no further treatment options for his advanced disease. Within the same session, he talked about travel plans for the following summer. When the therapist confronted him with the juxtaposition, the man replied: "Of course I am aware of the reality of my illness—and—I nonetheless hope for something better."

The patient may also be testing the therapist: "Which time framework will you buy? Or, can you tolerate the fluctuation which is the essence of my experience?" Adherence to child-time, to the exclusion of impinging reality, may signify fear and dysfunction. However, most families flow between the two sets of time, in a normal and adaptive process of maintaining hope. The therapist need only follow.

The Therapeutic Relationship

"What does that mean—'tame'?" [asked the little prince].

"It is an act too often neglected," said the fox. "It means to establish ties. . . ."

"What must I do, to tame you?" asked the little prince.

"You must be very patient," replied the fox. "First you will sit down at a little distance from me. . . . I shall look at you out of the corner of my eye and you will say nothing. But you will sit a little closer to me every day. . . . You become responsible, forever, for what you have tamed."   (Saint-Exupéry, 1971, p. 80 f.)

Such is the essence of the relationship between the individual with a life-threatening illness and the therapist. The therapist's role for the patient is highly specific: he or she is an anchoring presence in a life situation which otherwise feels unstable and vulnerable. The feelings which the patient projects on the therapist (transference) and those of the therapist for the patient (countertransference) come to mirror the themes of attachment and loss which the patient is confronting in every relationship.

In any psychotherapy, the transference is the crucial vehicle for exploration, since it is a prototype of the patient's development and functioning. With the urgency of life-threatening illness, an intense transference brings powerful emotions into high relief. However, the luxury of operating exclusively within the transference metaphor simply does not exist. Rather, the therapist must constantly translate back to the patient's "outside" life. That is, a close correspondence between the transference material and its implications for the patient's key relationships with family, friends, or other caregivers, must be maintained. One strives to foster a transference whose depth and intensity can fuel the tasks of living so crucial for someone with a limited life span.

In the following excerpt, a six-year-old child initiates a dialogue with his therapist, culminating in a profound revelation of his own sense of vulnerability.

Child: Did you ever have bad dreams?

18

Therapist: Yes, sometimes I have had bad dreams. Usually when I have bad dreams, it means that I'm worried about something.

Child: What are your bad dreams, usually?

Therapist: I think that they are a bit like yours. You know, monsters and things like that.

Child: And snakes. . . .

Therapist: What else do you have bad dreams about?

Child: A snake biting. . . .

Therapist: When you have those bad dreams, what do you think you are worried about?

Child: You dying. Everyone dying in the world and leaving me alone.

It is the very intensity and security of the therapeutic relationship which permits such candor. In turn, the agenda is set for exploring the patient's sense of overwhelming loss in all significant relationships.

In traditional psychotherapy, the patient's contact with the therapist is strictly limited to the session itself. Thus, the therapist has little "real" identity for the patient beyond this boundary. In an interdisciplinary setting where the therapist functions as a team member, such anonymity is rarely preserved. This "demystification" adds a level of complexity to the therapeutic relationship, whereby the projective nature of the transference intertwines with the reality of the alliance.

A patient overheard several nurses discussing the approaching marriage of the therapist who worked on the unit. His reaction was to panic in fear of "losing" her to her new commitment. Furthermore, at the time he was dealing with difficulties in his own marriage which had been exacerbated by his illness. The

19

therapist's control over a propitious time to disclose her situation to the patient (if at all) had been inadvertently preempted.

An aspect of the countertransference which is aroused particularly in those who work with the fatally ill is the "rescue fantasy" experienced by the therapist (Sourkes, 1977). In wanting to protect the vulnerable individual, the therapist encounters the danger of overinvolvement, a loss of boundary and role. By moving in to achieve a great deal of closeness with the patient, the therapist may in fact supplant the family by becoming a surrogate. The pitfalls of the "family surrogate" approach are evident for the patient and family as well.

The patient may feel threatened by an inordinate closeness to the therapist, while at the same time welcoming and needing the relationship. He or she feels trapped: "having to choose" between family and family surrogate, with a simultaneous fear of alienating either. The therapist must prevent the patient from ever experiencing such a forced choice position. One safeguard is to be found in the interpretation of the transference material. If the patient understands that the intense feelings which develop toward the therapist also have meaning for his or her other relationships, the sense of threat is minimized.

The family could feel estranged and supplanted just at the time they are desperately trying to "keep" the patient. Their pain is only exacerbated if they feel that the therapist is "better" than they in achieving closeness. The therapist and other caregivers must be aware of their own feelings of competition: such rivalry often serves as a danger signal of inappropriate involvement, coupled with a family's difficulty in relating to the patient.

Psychotherapy

The discussion at a case conference focused on a man's inadequate support of his wife during her prolonged hospitalization. The staff noted the husband's infrequent visits, and his discomfort in his wife's presence. Both the therapist and the nurses described their closeness to the patient. It was at this point that the therapist realized the staff's error: all were vying for a "special relationship" with the woman to compensate for the apparent problems within her marriage. Furthermore, the husband's behavior was clearly an indication of his own difficulty in coping with his wife's illness. The therapist was able to highlight these issues in the conference, and subsequent work focused on the couple's relationship.

The therapist often becomes a facilitator: one who makes easier, smoother, and more meaningful preexisting family relationships. The therapist can then move in and out of the family, tied exclusively neither to the patient nor to the other family members. By avoiding the "surrogate" role, the therapist flows with the system, strengthening and enhancing the structure of the family.

2

Life-Cycle Issues

*Life is so strange. Sometimes you feel it's like
  a book with chapters to fill, never ending.
Sometimes it's like a chess game where you have
  to make each move so carefully.
Other times it's like a mystery where each hidden
  chamber reveals its secrets.
It is even a war where to live it is to win it.*
  —Karen Beth Josephson, age 10

WHILE FEW PEOPLE ACTUALLY LIVE WITH THE SERENITY of "to everything there is a season," many hope for a life fabric into which events may be meaningfully woven. A diagnosis of life-threatening illness shatters the orderly and predictable unfolding of time. The degree and type of stress engendered for the patient, family and caregiver often depend upon what point the patient has reached in the life cycle.

The *elderly* patient has already lived a lifetime prior to the diagnosis. However, even to a person who has viewed approaching mortality with some equanimity, the diagnosis brings what was covert into overtly sharp focus. It is as a message of inevitability that the diagnosis is a crisis. For some elderly individuals, the satisfaction of completion can mitigate the impact of the diagnosis. In turn, the family and caregiver participate in caring for a person whose basic outlook remains positive. However, for many of the elderly, the fears of isolation and abandonment—all too often a reality—acutely counterbalance the comfort of closure. The caregiver may join the family in a neglectful stance, with the rationalization that the patient has already far outlived his or her time. Or, in reaction to such an attitude on the part of the family, the caregiver may take on excessive involvement with the patient.

The *young or middle-aged adult* confronted with life-threatening illness experiences the sense of being stopped short. In the words of one man: "You feel as if a knife just chopped you in half, so you can only make tentative gestures

25

and send out little tentacles for fear it may happen again." Just as the individual is planning and fulfilling life goals, the open horizons of the future are sharply delimited. The diagnosis sends reverberations through the adult's family of origin (parents and siblings) as well as through the nuclear family (spouse and children).

My children and . . . [my wife] have got to be cared for. To think of them alone without me is the fear that grips me through the nights. The thought of never seeing my children grow up haunts me more than anything. (Ryan and Ryan, 1979, p. 125)

Similarly, the diagnosis has an emotional impact on those who work with the patient. "This could be happening to me." Such is the painful awareness which confronts the caregiver of the adult patient and family. When the caregiver is of the same age and sex as the patient, or shares a common background, the likelihood of identification is increased. How does the caregiver handle this intensity? At one extreme, he or she may retreat dramatically from the patient in response to overwhelming anxiety. At the other extreme, the caregiver's inflated sense of sameness ("I know just how the patient feels, because I know how I would feel in that situation") may lead to inappropriate involvement.

Optimally, the caregiver develops an integrated sense of identification which can enrich his or her empathy for the patient and family's experience.

A twenty-year-old nursing student had an amputation immediately following diagnosis. During this surgical admission, she claimed that the nurses were avoiding her, and were particularly hostile to her requests for pain medication. In a case conference,

26

the nurses described the patient as being "immature" and "off the wall with anxiety." Eventually, they focused on their difficulty in witnessing someone *so like themselves* go through such devastation. The woman's requests for pain medication reminded the nurses of her anguish, and—by identification—of their own vulnerability. With the acknowledgment of these feelings, the nurses' anxiety and anger abated. Their identification with the patient, once a threat to be battled, instead became an asset in the caregiving relationship.

A *child or adolescent* diagnosed with a life-threatening illness throws an assumed sequence out of order. A time of role reversal is expected, when children will care for dying parents. When parents instead find themselves watching their child face death, a sense of tragic absurdity prevails. Not only is time shortened, but its order is shattered.

A child or adolescent with a life-threatening illness represents a premature separation to the family. Even before the child has become a differentiated individual through a natural developmental sequence, that child is wrenched away. There is little preparation for separation by death when a psychological separation has not yet been effected. The adolescent who is beginning to negotiate an independent existence is often the hardest to face when that "moving forward" is irreversibly halted, or at least disrupted. A child has not even had the time to begin to form life goals (Sourkes, 1977).

Younger children are not developed in themselves yet, in their own persons, in their own individualism. They can still be with their mother. Older people are away from their mother; they're detached, more adult. When you're in the middle, parents don't want to let you go. You want to be set free a little bit, but you want

27

to be able to come back. I just felt that I was denied any sort of chance. . . . Instead, it was decided for me: "You are going to mature very fast right now. You have to make life and death decisions. You have to accept things that children who are young adults between the ages of thirteen and nineteen don't normally have to face." It's like: "Grow up right now and become what you have to become to deal with this." I never had the chance to be sweet sixteen. I never had the chance to be gay old seventeen. I had to automatically be an adult, and it was very hard."

In the context of talking pensively about his illness, a five-year-old child commented to his therapist: "It takes a lot of days to be grown up, doesn't it. . . ."

The caregiver often identifies with the parents of a pediatric patient. This reaction intensifies when the caregiver is also a parent, especially if his or her healthy child is of the same age as the patient. For the caregiver who does not yet have children, the spectre of a fatally ill child may loom threateningly. Furthermore, to witness a child endure pain evokes enormous guilt and helplessness in the family and caregiver alike.

An oncologist remarked that he could never work with pediatric patients. "I can tolerate seeing pain and disfigurement, but not when those bruised bodies and bald heads belong to children."

What is the underlying anxiety common to all individuals facing a life-threatening illness? It is the fear that life will end before he or she has had the chance to live it as planned. As one woman stated: "I feel like a watch that is winding down." The patient senses allotted time running out, in the direction of irreversible finality.

28

3

Loss

I know the purity of pure despair.
—Theodore Roethke

AS THE THEMATIC FRAMEWORK for the experience of life-threatening illness, loss can be conceptualized along three intersecting axes: loss of control, loss of identity, and loss of relationships. These dimensions emerge in slightly different form throughout the trajectory of the illness, from the time of diagnosis until their ultimate realization at the moment of death.

Loss of Control

Loss of control is a pivotal issue, not to say fear, of the individual confronting life-threatening illness. In the moment of diagnosis, one's entire sense of control dissolves in coming face-to-face with the limits of finite time. The patient experiences loss of control in many areas: over his or her body, over disease and pain, over emotional boundaries, and ultimately over life itself. The unknown lies ahead like an uncharted chasm, without landmarks or guide. Learning to live with a life-threatening illness is thus a constant adaptation to tolerating risk and the unknown. As Bell (1961) reflected about his own illness: "By writing down what is happening to me . . . I can to some degree control it. At least, when and if it does happen, it won't catch me altogether by surprise. I won't be moving blindly into a darkness filled with unknown terrors. I'll have been there before" (p. 4). The antidote to an overriding sense of loss of control is for the patient to take an

31

active, responsible stance toward the illness: "What can *I* do to prolong and enrich *my* life?" To know that one is doing something—no matter how limited—can have powerful impact. It is not uncommon for the patient who feels overwhelmed to consider suicide as an option. However, even with the expression of suicidal ideation, it is rare that the individual resorts to this ultimate act.

The very nature of illness makes a person vulnerable to a sense of loss of control. Along with disease comes the realization that something in one's body has ceased to function and has gone awry. Bodily processes which were always taken for granted are suddenly in question. With the proliferation of abnormal cells in malignant disease, loss of control translates from the microscopic level to the patient's actual experience: it is as if the brakes have failed. The fact that many diseases can be shown to recur in the absence of manifest symptoms only augments the patient's anxiety. There is a constant lurking question of what is *really* happening inside one's body, even when everything appears well. The symptoms and pain of the illness, as well as the side effects of treatment, often seem to overtake the very being of the individual. Thus patients talk about the sense of repeated assault, much like being powerless against the elements.

A woman who would experience intense nausea and vomiting even before receiving her chemotherapy explained: "I keep telling myself that these are only medicines, and that I'm a person, and they shouldn't get the better of me. But something comes over me when I walk into the clinic and I just give up."

A child recounted feeling like "a piece of paper that everyone cuts into" whenever he was hospitalized.

Self-help techniques, including relaxation, guided imagery, and hypnosis form an integral part of the therapeutic approach. They can be powerful tools in the control of anxiety, nausea, and pain. Regardless of the actual impact of such techniques on symptoms, most patients report an increased sense of well-being at their perception of exerting control.

Paradoxically, the caregiving system itself often reinforces the patient's sense of limited control. Individual autonomy and options tend to have low priority in a hospital or clinic setting. This is a grim disappointment for the patient who seeks individual recognition and stability within the caregiving environment.

A young woman wore old, shabby clothes whenever she came into the clinic for chemotherapy. She commented spontaneously one day: "If I got sick and were wearing my nice regular clothes, I would never want to wear them again. They would always remind me of my illness."

By such graphic containment, this woman is controlling the intrusion of the illness into her life. She is responding to the sense, so often expressed by patients, that the illness *is* their life, rather than just a part of it. Caregivers often refer to "the angry patient": a stereotypically hostile, noncompliant individual who lashes out at any overture or assistance. Too often the source of that anger goes unrecognized. For, in most cases, "the angry patient" is having inordinate difficulty coping with the loss of control wrought by the illness. Once the meaning of this anger is acknowledged and the caregiving environment structured to allow for as much control as feasible, the patient's behavior changes dramatically. If an individual masters small situations, he or she feels an increased sense of control over the ultimate.

Loss of control over emotional boundaries emerges as an issue particularly during hospitalization. The patient experiences a continual ambivalence: while desperately wanting to be surrounded by people, he or she may also long for privacy. When the individual is immobile, there is no way to exit for space. Furthermore, it is rare that the patient asks visitors to leave; to send someone away is much too threatening. Thus, unless family and staff are sensitive to cues, the patient may experience a sense of engulfment, of vanished boundaries.

Under the enormous stress of illness, the patient may regress to earlier levels of expression and coping. Emotional flexibility—whereby the individual allows him or herself to be truly vulnerable, accepting fear and dependence—can be highly functional during certain periods. Such regression is normal, and redresses itself as the crisis abates.

The constant shift in levels of control thus pervades the experience of life-threatening illness. In order to avoid the trap of all-or-nothing extremes, the individual strives for balance in exerting and relinquishing control. Within the framework of the illness, such adaptation enables the patient to structure meaningful priorities for living.

Loss of Identity

A man goes far to find out what he is.
—Theodore Roethke

Such is the search for identity, for an integrated sense of self. While an individual's identity may broaden to incorpo-

34

rate new facets, its essential configuration remains constant over time. What, then, are the implications of life-threatening illness for one's sense of identity? Initially the diagnosis is viewed as an external intruder. The patient refers to "*the* illness, *the* cancer" as if to assert: "This illness is separate from me." Over time, the patient begins to speak quite naturally of "*my* illness, *my* cancer," or even of "being leukemic" rather than "having leukemia." These subtle shifts in language are testimony to a significant process: what began as an external entity has been transformed into an internalized part of one's physical and emotional being. The task is to create a balance whereby an individual's identity as a patient is incorporated into the broader spectrum.

The feared loss of identity is captured in a patient's statement: "I'm afraid of changing so much with this disease that I won't recognize myself." The term "catastrophic illness" is never more applicable than when addressing issues of identity. For the patient experiences reverberations of earthquake proportion: "Who was I, and what is left of me now?" The pervasive fear is of being defined exclusively in terms of the illness, both by oneself and by others.

Physical manifestations of the illness often have major impact on the individual's sense of identity. Compounding the patient's own difficulty in adjusting to an altered body image is the fear of others' shock and revulsion at his or her appearance. At a more hidden level, an illness which affects sexuality directly through symptoms and effects of treatment, or indirectly through general debilitation, can be particularly devastating. Most profoundly, physical changes, whether obvious or subtle, attest to the presence of disease, and so to the threat of loss.

The Deepening Shade

I didn't like what the tumor had done to the architecture of my body. . . . What distressed me was the significance rather than the ugliness of what I saw; and what I saw was the utter gravity of my illness, visible and palpable, not to be ignored or argued away. My doom made flesh.   (Bell, 1961, p. 16)

So often the patient feels alone: alone with pain, fear, and most basic, the identity of being one who is sick. For a newly diagnosed patient to meet someone who has gone through treatment and returned to "normal" functioning can have salutary impact. Patients unite in the struggle which transcends differences in other aspects of their lives. Whatever support is garnered from family and caregivers, there is a unique credibility which only another patient can offer.

Cancer patients have a bond that surpasses a healthy person's understanding. The presence of fear and the agony of pain are transmitted without words from one of us to another. I cannot say how this is done. I only know it happens.

(Ryan and Ryan, 1979, p. 345)

Yet overall it is critical that the individual maintain his or her lifelong identity intact. Very often a patient who becomes severely depressed after diagnosis fears a total shattering of that identity in exchange for becoming "a dying patient." During such periods when the patient's sense of identity falters under the weight of the illness, ongoing affirmation by the family and caregiver is particularly crucial. As the patient gradually assimilates the illness into his or her overall identity, the depression lessens.

The identity of being a patient with a life-threatening illness has interesting implications for the issue of denial

36

(Sourkes, 1976). The internalized recognition of illness explains why the individual can never slip completely into denial without a real "identity crisis." That is, "to lose" the illness through denial would be "to lose" an integral part of one's identity. Family members often do not understand this internalization, and simply see the illness as a defined set of physical symptoms. Thus, in the absence of symptoms, they tend to erase the illness from their view of the patient.

This aspect also relates to how a prolonged remission, or cure, demands profound identity reorganization of the patient. As a young adult wrote: "I am caught in a limbo. What made me happy/what I wanted before the cancer, and what will make me happy/what I want now that I'm rid of the cancer, don't seem tangible things anymore." This statement attests to the agony of adapting one's identity to changing life-death circumstances, even when the direction is salutary.

Loss of Relationships

Therapist: What does it mean to be alive?
Child: That your family doesn't miss you. They miss you if you die. When you're alive, you don't miss people because they are right here.

Absence—physical, psychological, and social—connotes profound and total emptiness. This element lies at the crux of loss of relationships. While issues of control and identity belong primarily to the patient, the loss of relationships is shared from mirror image perspective by both patient and family. All are grappling with the inevitable transformation of presence ("they are right here") into absence ("they miss you if you die"). Whereas absence is a part of every loss, an undercurrent of isolation and abandonment is not. Such a threatening sense of severed bonds often signifies a family devastated by the impact of the illness. It is the continuum of presence-absence which provides the defining structure for loss of relationships.

It's no privilege having someone with cancer in your family. Of all the things I ever could have chosen, having someone in my family get cancer is not one of them.

This child speaks for anyone whose family is affected by life-threatening illness. Whatever the relationship—marital, parent-child or sibling—the sense of impending absence is pervasive. Only its manifestation differs as a function of the type of relationship. Between spouses, the essential loss is that of a life companion. The fear most often voiced is that of being alone: for the patient, alone in death; for the spouse, alone in the future. For the child whose parent is ill, the critical concern is for care and protection: What will become of me? Who will be there for me? The parent is racked by the anguish of being unable to provide the security of ongoing presence for that child. When a child is the patient, both parents and child are gripped in a separation struggle against the threat of death. The sibling focuses on a sense of fearful identification (could this also happen to me?) and the loss of a person so like himself or herself. Overall, the ramifications of the illness will vary depending on the preexisting quality of these relationships. Salient dimensions include: closeness-distance, independence-dependence, and flexibility-rigidity of the family structure.

Relationships which do not fit a clear family category are often overlooked by the caregiving staff. Thus, while a friend may be closer to the patient than any relative, that individual is rarely accorded comparable recognition and support. For a patient whose primary relationship is in transition at the time of the diagnosis, powerful dilemmas may arise. For example, a woman engaged to be married cried despairingly: "How can I marry my fiancé and then die on him?" Individuals in the process of a divorce are thrown into anguished confusion as to which direction to pursue in the face of ultimate separation. Whatever the nature of the transition, its existence intensifies the sense of threatened loss.

Within the context of loss of relationships, sexuality is a central concern. The reassurance of touch may be sought by both partners as an antidote to their impending loss; yet, all too often, it is that very intimacy which is missing. The patient's physical debilitation, or the specific nature of the illness, may preclude sexual functioning. However, psychological reasons are often paramount in explaining a couple's abstinence. Some couples, despite all reassurance to the contrary, fear contagion of the disease through sexual contact. Or the spouse may consider the patient too fragile and thus hesitate to initiate lovemaking. When the spouse and the patient view themselves as moving in different directions—one toward life, the other toward death—the meaning of lovemaking may be too painful. Most common, a couple may feel that a bridge between them has been severed during the patient's prolonged hospitalizations, when there has been little occasion for privacy and closeness. On the patient's return home, physical intimacy must be rebuilt and nurtured. To compound the problem, it is rare that caregivers raise the issue of sexuality with the patient. Thus, what begins as a temporary problem all too often develops into an ever-widening breach between the couple. When a child is the patient, parents often describe a lessening of their sexual functioning. Much of their energy is being funneled into the care of the child, and in many cases, sexuality becomes linked with the guilt of having produced a child who may die. In all of these circumstances, the pervasive theme is of how lovemaking stirs up sadness, how in the midst of such acute presence, the intimacy bespeaks absence.

The role changes which occur as a consequence of the illness are another area of stress for the family. When the patient is the primary wage-earner and must give up work, a crucial aspect of his or her identity is lost. Furthermore, this individual becomes increasingly dependent on the other family members at a time when their emotional resources are taxed. Financial strain creates tension and conflict, both in coping with the present, and in fears for the future. The patient may feel enormous guilt at "causing" these difficulties to the point where his or her will to live may be affected. All too often, the caregiver relegates a family's financial concerns to the hospital credit office without recognizing the overriding psychological dimensions of the problem. Other types of role change may also have profound impact on a family structure. For example, when one parent is ill, the children begin to turn more to the other parent for their day-to-day care. Or, an individual previously dependent on the spouse for many decisions suddenly finds and acts with a new independence when that spouse takes ill. These shifts, while necessary and at times positive for an individual's development, nonetheless take an emotional toll. Their reverberations contribute significantly to the family's omnipresent sense of loss.

Interventions which preserve the bridge between the patient and family also maintain each individual's sense of self-worth. During hospitalizations, the family's participation in caregiving assuages their helplessness, while assuring the patient of their involvement. As a further sign of presence, the family can be encouraged to use touch in comforting the patient. At home, it is important that the patient continue in his or her accustomed roles to whatever extent is feasible. When necessary, different or more limited roles can be created to accommodate the exigencies of the illness. Indeed, support for the entire family is critical, whether it be from relatives, friends, or community resources. Self-help groups may be valuable settings in which families can share experiences. Most fundamental of all, the patient and family seek meaning in their own belief system—religious, philosophical, or interpersonal —as a structure for coping with loss.

4

Diagnosis

I remember a stone breaking the eddying current. . . .
A vulnerable place,
Surrounded by sand, broken shells, the wreckage of
    water.

                                    —*Theodore Roethke*

THE DIAGNOSIS OF A LIFE-THREATENING ILLNESS cata-
pults the patient and family into an irreversibly altered reality.
Regardless of which aspects of life appear unchanged, in fact,
nothing is the same. The events surrounding the diagnosis
are indelibly imprinted in the memory of the patient and
family. It is as if time stopped, and the images were frozen
at a standstill. Although the prognosis for certain diseases
may hold new optimism, the subjective experience of receiving the diagnosis still connotes death. Thus it is not altogether
surprising that in the years after the patient's death, family
members often comment that the date of diagnosis is as
powerful an anniversary as the actual date of death.

Much attention has been devoted in the past to the impact
of telling versus not telling the diagnosis and prognosis to
the patient and family. More crucial now is the dilemma:
how does one impart such knowledge? The following statements attest to the inherent difficulty:

How does one tell a bright twelve-year-old that he has a "life-
threatening" disease?   (Rappaport, 1980, p. 110)

A woman recounted with great resentment how the surgeon had
told her the diagnosis while he was taking out her stitches: "He
had me turn my face to the wall so that he wouldn't have to look
at me."

Tests were performed and the next morning my doctor informed
me I had acute leukemia. I was alone. . . . I've often wondered

45

whether there would have been a better way to tell me. I've decided there is no good way to be told you're going to die.

(Jaffe, 1975, p. 37)

The stress experienced by the patient and family on hearing the verdict is more often documented than that of the caregiver who must deliver the diagnosis. This enormous burden may be magnified by the magical thinking on the part of some patients and families that "in telling the diagnosis, you give the disease."

An orthopedic surgeon insisted on having another member of the caregiving team present when he told adolescents that they would need an amputation. He acknowledged his need to share the devastation of "telling" when he then had to perform such a mutilative procedure.

The mother of a pediatric patient explained: "I hated the doctor who told us. He was the bearer of bad news, and I felt as if the diagnosis were his fault."

Bowen (1976) refers to the "emotional shock wave" phenomenon: "A network of underground 'aftershocks' of serious life events that can occur anywhere in the extended family system in the months or years following serious emotional events in a family. It occurs most often after the death or the *threatened death* of a significant family member" (p. 339, italics added). Open communication around the crisis of diagnosis may at least partly defuse the shock wave's reverberations.

In optimal circumstances, a family member is present when the patient is told the diagnosis. If the family has been informed ahead of time, any delay in telling the patient can become a source of unease and mistrust. The patient will sense the altered emotional climate, without having the facts to interpret the change. It is similarly important that there be no discrepancy between what the patient and family are told. Certain families (particularly with an ill child) choose to tell the patient themselves, and then have a caregiver enter.

Demystification—the lifting of the mysterious and the unknown—is a primary goal in communicating the diagnosis. Candor, reassurance, and realistic hope are its essential components. Information must be presented in clear, simple language. Too often, under high anxiety, the caregiver retreats to the protection of medical terminology, leaving the patient lost in the process. Given the shock of diagnosis, the individual can absorb only a limited amount of information at the outset. Thus, the caregiver must present the facts slowly, in incremental steps. The patient can ask for more data as he or she feels ready, thereby experiencing a sense of mastery and control. In most cases, the patient must sign a consent form which names the diagnosis and details the risks and benefits of the proposed treatment. Intended as a factual document, its emotional impact for the patient cannot be underestimated. For it stands as written confirmation of his or her vulnerablity.

While it is usually the physician who tells the diagnosis, he or she can garner support from the presence of other caregivers. Furthermore, the patient and family witness interdisciplinary team functioning, an approach which provides them with a sense of security from the start. The therapist's role is to observe reactive patterns within the family; to monitor the flow of discussion; and in some instances, to remain with the family after the physician's departure. However, it is crucial to be sensitive to a family's need to be alone in sharing their grief after hearing the diagnosis.

Family members not present at the initial conference must be offered the opportunity to meet with the physician. It is also critical that the factual and emotional content of the meeting be communicated to staff who will be involved in the patient's care. Such a network ensures congruity and trust among the patient, family, and caregiving team.

A family may insist that the diagnosis be hidden from the patient, stating that he or she "won't be able to take it." In most cases, the family is responding to their own devastation and grief, and projecting it on the patient. It is crucial that the caregiver not storm the family's resistance; for all too often, an alliance is then ruptured before it has even developed. Once given the chance to discuss their own fear, most families are amenable and equipped to face the patient. There are families whose cultural or religious beliefs or closed style of communication absolutely dictate against such disclosure. In these difficult circumstances, the physician may have to serve as the patient's advocate and take a stand contrary to the family's wishes.

Coexistent with a medical understanding of the diagnosis, many individuals cling to a "private" interpretation of its meaning. This version may be fraught with elements of fear, guilt, and magical thinking. Or, the diagnosis may be imbued with some "higher reason," in order to be integrated into a salutary belief system. In either case, the attribution of meaning to the diagnosis indicates a powerful need to make sense of the incomprehensible.

48

Diagnosis

A woman diagnosed with ovarian cancer cried repetitively: "How could I have caused myself to get cancer in that place?" She then talked about her sexual history, with particular focus on an abortion which she had had years previously.

An adolescent said of her sister's diagnosis: "I think maybe it was God's way of telling our family to pull together. There had been a lot of dissension among us, and maybe this was a way to bring us together."
                                                            (Sourkes, 1980)

In response to a child's query: "Why did I get this disease, and not some robber or something?" her mother replied: "God would only give it to a strong person like you who can fight it."

With a diagnosis established, the patient enters the initial phase of treatment, often frightening and invasive. In a matter of days or weeks, the patient may feel sicker than ever before. During this period, caregivers frequently refer to a patient's "denial": he or she is not talking about the illness. What must be recognized is that in the battle to survive the onslaught of treatment, psychological energy is a luxury. Rarely is the patient denying the illness, a fact almost precluded by the very bombardment of his or her body. Rather, the individual may be actively choosing *not* to deal with the implications of the diagnosis when all available energy is needed for physical survival. Such selective attention can be highly adaptive. Related to the "overdiagnosis" of denial during the acute phase is the confusion of withdrawal with depression in the patient's behavior:

When I'm physically drained, I often don't feel like talking. . . . Many times in the hospital I'm not depressed, though I may seem withdrawn. I'm concentrating all my energies on just handling the

49

physical aspects. . . . It's like a runner out of breath—I need to catch my breath and not dissipate energy.

(Jaffe, Jaffe, and Love, 1976)

It wasn't that I felt desperately ill physically, or even desperately depressed. I felt, instead, a kind of weariness, a vast indifference. In my head during this time there was a sort of continual background music—or rather, background cacaphony—not exactly a headache, but a kind of murmuring unpleasantness.

(Alsop, 1973, p. 125)

Another feeling which may be mistaken for depression is sadness: the patient's grief for the losses incurred by the diagnosis. Whereas it is rare for the diagnosis to precipitate a clinical depression, reactions of withdrawal and sadness are to be expected.

A physician prescribed an antidepressant for a young man who had been hospitalized for several weeks following diagnosis. The patient refused the medication angrily: "I don't need that stuff. Why can't you just let me be sad for awhile? How else do you expect me to feel when I'm this sick, look awful, and might have to spend Christmas in the hospital?" As the man began to feel better physically, his mood in turn lifted. He commented to his physician: "I told you just to give me time."

During the diagnostic phase, the family functions as an indivisible unit aginst the threat of diminution. In extremity, there is little space for individual ebb and flow. Rather, a tight circle around family members constricts their outward movement, binding them to the focus of the crisis. Individuals are "in sync" with one another, feeling and thinking alike. Such fusion is highly adaptive under stress: decision making and

Diagnosis

the articulation of feelings are facilitated by the shared focus.

The diagnosis thus stands as the prologue to the unfolding of life-threatening illness. Existence is stripped to the essence. In the words of one individual: "There's live, or there's die, and I'm going to live." The caregiver must now facilitate the transition from the immediate crisis of diagnosis into the chronic phase, an interval of new stress and complexity.

5

Neutral Time

Time folds into a long moment.
—Theodore Roethke

THE LIVING-DYING INTERVAL reflects the prolonged duration of remission and survival in many forms of life-threatening illness. In the past, the illness trajectory moved directly from diagnosis to death, with little intervening time or space. This "new" middle phase can unfold in many guises: a cycle of remissions and relapses, a gradual downhill course, or prolonged remission implying cure. Whatever its precise nature, it is this interval which has made the word "terminal" inapplicable much of the time. When a person lives for months or years—albeit with a diagnosis implying premature mortality —"terminal" loses its impact. The slow leave-taking may be better characterized by "life-threatening" or "chronic," terms with less sense of a fixed endpoint. The challenge which faces the patient and family is to maintain a semblance of normal life in the "abnormal" presence of life-threatening illness.

"Neutral time" describes the subjective experience of the living-dying interval. The individual lives in a state of limbo, wherein the only certainty is, paradoxically, uncertainty. There is a sense of being suspended in space and time, without defined movement in either a forward or backward direction. The projective nature of neutral time means that the individual can imbue it with different meanings and choose to move actively within it. However, as a state of being, neutral time is the inescapable framework of the period.

> So much of adolescence is an ill-defined dying,
> An intolerable waiting,

55

The Deepening Shade

A longing for another place and time,
Another condition.

(Theodore Roethke)

Although these lines were written to describe adolescence, they are palpably evocative of the experience of living in neutral time. "An ill-defined dying" connotes that suspended limbo when death looms potential or imminent. "An intolerable waiting" captures the essence of the living-dying interval; and is accompanied by the "longing" for relief, for another condition of being. The stress of waiting for an event which is inevitable, yet whose time of arrival is unknown, is enormous. As one family member said during the patient's prolonged illness: "I wonder whether I'll ever be able to wait for anything again." Bell (1961, p. 88) describes the sense of neutral time from the patient's point of view:

The mere fact of repetition . . . tends to invest my life with a false normality, so that now and then I catch myself thinking there's no reason why I shouldn't go on like this for a long time. As if the unnatural had become the normal and dying a way of life. . . . I've been dying for months now, but how long can I go on being afraid of something that doesn't happen? I was not dead yesterday, I am not dead today, so why shouldn't I be not dead tomorrow as well?

The transition from the acute diagnostic phase into the more chronic period of the illness frequently coincides with the patient's discharge from the hospital. While in some ways terrifying and alien, the hospital has nonetheless provided a cushion of security for the patient and family. In fact, after a prolonged admission, patients often refer to the hospital and

56

caregiving staff as a "second home and family." Thus, a certain ambivalence surrounds the leave-taking.

An adolescent girl left the following note at the nursing station on the day she was discharged: "I am leaving you. I'm sure you'll be glad to see me go, but I will be back, have no fear. If you happen to miss me, I'll be at home for awhile. You can reach me there. But please don't. I enjoy my privacy. Take care of my friends and allies on this ~~stated~~ sacred floor."

The homecoming sets up a frightening confrontation for both the patient and family. The familiarity of home—where on one level nothing has changed during the hospitalization —is now tinged by the presence of life-threatening illness. The relief and reunion of the homecoming are juxtaposed with a sense of change and anticipated loss. In a dramatic re-entry, the patient is thrust from the constricted universe of a hospital room into the wider world. Both patient and family are often apprehensive about the responsibility for the patient's care and safety. The patient questions whether he or she can resume former roles and lifestyles now that the diagnosis has intervened. However expressed, the terror is of living with an illness which has suddenly appeared in the family's midst.

Families can't function at crisis tempo forever. Chronic illness, no matter how bad, can and does become routine. . . . Routine means security; it dulls the feeling of danger. Somewhere in one's mind is the notion that since disaster and routine are incompatible concepts, we must be safe.   (Rappaport, 1980, p. 112)

With the abatement of the immediate crisis, the patient and

family members each look to pursue the individual pathways of "normal" life. In contrast to the fusion which characterized the diagnostic phase, a process of differentiation gradually emerges. Boundaries which had dissolved between individuals are reestablished, and the constrictive circle around the family resumes elasticity and permeability. The precise synchrony of feeling and thought gives way to the less intense homeostasis of daily life. Being "out of sync" with others in pursuing one's own physical and emotional space is now highly functional. Although the illness remains an enormous threat, it becomes an internalized force within the family system. Undergirding its presence is the emotional process of anticipatory grief. The rhythm of neutral time, of living with the ever present possibility of disease, may be shattered by the patient's relapse or unexpected death. In contrast, the elective cessation of treatment promises a more salutary future.

Elective Cessation of Treatment

Therapist: What has been your most frightening experience since diagnosis?

Patient: When the Doc told me I will not be taking any more medication.

Many patients are on a treatment program of specific duration, generally between six months and two years. If they remain free of disease throughout the course of treatment, their therapy is ended. The term "elective cessation" refers to the discontinuation of all forms of therapy at a time when the disease is judged to have been adequately treated. While the program may have included surgery and radiation therapy, in terms of elective cessation, chemotherapy is most often the issue. In the past, elective cessation of treatment was experienced by few patients, since most relapsed. However, with more individuals surviving for longer periods of time, this new and critical milestone has emerged.

The psychological crisis evoked by elective cessation reflects the inordinate ambivalence which surrounds the treatment process. On the one hand, the patient and family view chemotherapy as actively combating the threat of the illness: each dose is a step toward prevention or cure. Inextricable with its lifegiving attributes, however, are the negatives. The drugs are often invasive, causing enormous discomfort and complications, as well as disrupting the routine of daily life. Furthermore, each treatment is a reminder of the disease whose absence is never totally guaranteed.

At the outset, the patient and family focus on "getting through treatment," with much discussion of future plans for when it will be over. From the long-range perspective, they imbue the end of treatment with almost magical properties, as if it will mean certain cure and a return to normal life: an eradication of what has been. Over time, however, anxiety about its cessation begins to lurk. Tentative questions arise as to the wisdom of the patient "not getting anything." Queries about the possibility of relapse increase in frequency. The patient and family may inquire about continuing treatment with drugs of less toxicity. These concerns intermingle with expressions of relief at the approaching end of treatment. The crisis of elective cessation may thus be seen as the patient and family's confrontation with the loss of their life support. Although the balance of ambivalence varies both within and between individuals, its presence can almost always be detected.

An adult patient explained the conflict in the following words: "You hate every minute of getting those drugs; yet, paradoxically, as the end of treatment approaches, you wish they would continue giving them to you. It's like your lifeline."

A woman had a recurrent nightmare in the weeks around her last course of treatment: a man runs after her, threatening to kill her. Just when she thinks she is safe, he catches her.

To his physician and therapist, an adolescent expressed only eagerness to end chemotherapy so that his hair would grow back. However, he asked his parents whether he would experience "withdrawal" symptoms in coming off the drugs.

Preparation for the elective cessation of treatment is a critical therapeutic measure in working with the patient and family. Beginning months ahead of time, the physician and therapist should actively elicit discussion about its approach. The patient and family must be educated that the ending of treatment is *both* a positive milestone and a crisis and that ambivalence about it is the norm. The caregiver who has developed a relationship with them may also experience the mixture of elation and fear evoked by the end of treatment.

While giving a child her last dose of chemotherapy, the nurse said: "I'll miss seeing you every three weeks, but I won't miss giving you this stuff." After hugging the child, she turned to one of her colleagues and said: "And I hope she doesn't relapse now. . . ."

Neutral Time

Relapse

The threat of relapse is an ever present counterpoint to the hope for prolonged survival. The intensity which surrounds the remission-relapse cycle is reflected in a mother's statement: "When our child first got sick, we fought a battle to get him into remission. If he relapses now, after all this time, we'll fight a war." Disease may be shown to recur in the absence of any manifest symptoms, at a time that the patient looks and feels well. This teasing quality of many illnesses means that each routine examination engenders enormous anxiety: will this be the time that a relapse is discovered? Whether it takes minutes, hours, or days to obtain test results, the patient and family contemplate every possible contingency and outcome.

A marrow test is an unpleasant experience, and a biopsy is more so. But neither is nearly so unpleasant as waiting for the results. Every time I had a marrow test, there would be that hour or so of suspense, filled with the fear of a "fulmination" of the abnormal cells. The fulmination would be followed by chemotherapy, the laminar flow room, and the near-certainty of death in a year or two. (Alsop, 1973, p. 70)

The threat of relapse lends a pivot to the rhythm of the neutral time interval. Anticipation brings the family into a shared pervasive anxiety which binds them together until the "all-clear" signal is given for another period of time. The family's synchrony is thus in constant flux, structured in part by the procedures and events which accompany the illness:

The night before our son comes in for a bone marrow aspiration is always the same. He gets gloomy and goes to bed right after

61

dinner. My husband and I sleep fitfully, and each spends part of the night up reading or pacing. We are all caught in the same web of anxiety which breaks the instant we are told his bone marrow is fine.

What happens when a recurrence is discovered? The announcement to the patient and family triggers a grief reaction reminiscent of the time of initial diagnosis. The first relapse is particularly traumatic in that it changes the view of the illness trajectory. In most cases, it indicates that treatment toward cure has failed and that the chances of prolonged survival are diminished. Furthermore, the relapse shatters any budding hope that the nightmare of illness might be in the past. Even in cases where a recurrence does not preclude long-term survival, it still has enormous impact. With each subsequent relapse, the immediacy of the disease reasserts itself, translating the "possibility" of its presence into actuality. Thus, the relapse is a signal, a reminder that the patient may be living on borrowed time. For these reasons, it is often more difficult to inform the patient and family of a relapse than it was to communicate the original diagnosis. The caregiver who has developed a relationship with the patient and family must now contend with his or her own sadness at the relapse's foreboding implications.

The patient expresses anguish and outrage at a disease which returns just when life seemed to be redressing its balance. A sense of betrayal—by one's own body, by treatment, and by the caregiving team—is paramount.

An adolescent with leukemia who had just relapsed grieved: "This isn't how they told me it would be when I was diagnosed. If I had stayed in remission, I would be coming off treatment in a couple of months. Instead—look at me—just starting a whole new set of medicines which are not even as strong as the first ones."

The struggle to return the patient to remission can be arduous and painful, whatever the treatment modality. When surgery is indicated, for example, the patient dreads further bodily mutilation whose outcome may or may not be the eradication of disease. Inherent in the relapse phenomenon with regard to chemotherapy is the knowledge that despite a change of treatment plan, the likelihood of cure is greatly diminished. The drugs may, however, return the patient to remission. Reinduction can take weeks or months, with life-threatening complications a frequent accompaniment. The process is fraught with medical, psychological, and ethical issues. Foremost is the question: under what circumstances does one fight to attain remission? The patient and family must feel that there is a reasonable hope of this outcome and that the quality of time gained will be worthy of the struggle.

During the reinduction phase, it is critical that the family be in close synchrony with the patient, who often feels enormous ambivalence about the battle. On the one hand he or she may plead to be left alone, to give up; counterbalanced, if not outweighed, by the desire to keep trying, despite the hardship. The family members feel an awesome responsibility in "monitoring" this ebb and flow. They must support one another, compare perceptions of the patient's wishes, and plan for contingencies of whether or not the patient attains remission. When patients do go into remission after a prolonged struggle, they often express gratitude that their pleas to be left alone were not heeded literally by the family and caregiving team.

The Deepening Shade

Unexpected Death

Unexpected death occurs when the patient dies of infection or drug toxicity without evidence of malignant disease. Such a death is particularly painful when it occurs during a first remission, a time when hope for prolonged survival or cure rides high. The tragic irony of unexpected death catches the family off guard. Although they have known that death might result from infection or drug complications, their preoccupation has been the disease itself. The family often reacts with intense anger, guilt, and shaken trust in the caregiving team and institution. The grieving process is complicated by their attempt somehow "to justify" what the patient went through. Other patients on the same protocol may experience enormous ambivalence about continuing treatment. The impact on caregiving staff is also profound and provokes much self-questioning and discussion about the relative benefits and risks of the protocol. In disease entities where treatment might have been curative, the unexpected death during remission is the ultimate blow for both family and caregiver.

6

Anticipatory Grief

All things rolling away from me,
All shapes, all stones.
                    —Theodore Roethke

ANTICIPATORY GRIEF IS THE PROCESS which links individuals facing loss. It is catapulted into being at the time of diagnosis, and wends its way through the living-dying interval until the moment of death. Anticipatory grief initially resembles the grief which immediately follows a death: emotions are alternately raw and numb, and very much in evidence. Its most complex dimensions are played out in the interval of neutral time. In contrast to its almost palpable presence at diagnosis, anticipatory grief now charts a subterranean course as the undergirding and pervasive theme of the living-dying experience.

Grief had come to join our team. We would be able to push it away from time to time, although never for long—and the crucible was still to come, somewhere ahead, awaiting us.

(Ryan and Ryan, 1979, p. 32)

Anticipatory grief is defined as "grief expressed in advance when the loss is perceived as inevitable" (Aldrich, 1974, p. 4). Experientially the process reflects the emotional response to the pain of separation prior to the actuality of loss. The patient grieves multiple losses: of self, of loved ones, of all that has been important in his or her life. It is not oblivion itself which is feared so much as the separation from those who love and nurture. The awareness of being alone in facing the unknown is acutely heightened.

I see certain things happening and I allow certain things to happen that indicate I recognize that separation coming. A few weeks ago

The Deepening Shade

I was upstairs taking a rest and . . . [my husband and daughter] were downstairs . . . and I all of a sudden felt this extreme detachment and separation from the two of them. I came downstairs and I sat on the stairs. . . . They didn't see me. I watched them and it was really a weird experience because . . . it was like I wasn't there.   (Bresloff, Bresloff, and Goodyear, 1975)

The family members face anticipatory grief, and then bereavement after the patient dies. They move from the realization: "The patient is going to die" to an even more anguished dawning: "We are going to lose the patient." It is at this juncture that the family's anticipatory grief shifts from a focus on the patient to a sense of their own inner loss. No matter how close the relationship between the patient and family, an inevitable separation has begun.

From the time of diagnosis, the patient lives with a sense of borrowed time. He or she is grateful for the temporary certainty of each day, within the overall context of uncertainty. The individual uses the time to "finish unfinished business"; a thrust toward completion permeates all avenues of life. For this reason, it is important that a patient have the right to know his or her diagnosis and prognosis. The information can provide a time context within which to organize— and reorganize—priorities. The individual's initial reaction to confronting time limits may be either frenetic activity or immobilization: where to begin? The therapist can play a critical role in helping the patient formulate a hierarchy of life tasks, thereby immediately instilling a sense of control over time. Such structure is also important for the family, both for the present and in preparing for new roles which lie ahead.

The family's focus is thus on beginnings which emerge from completion.

For both the patient and family, there is no longer the luxury of "waiting for the perfect moment"; opportunity must be actively created, not passively awaited. It is a time for the exchange of shared feelings, of the appreciations and resentments which have accrued over a lifetime. In working through the separation process, the expression of both positive and negative feelings is necessary. However, the patient and family may find it too dangerous to express anger or hostility during this vulnerable period. The patient fears alienating the family, who in turn harbor an almost magical belief that their anger could harm the patient. Reassurance by the therapist that all meaningful relationships entail a degree of ambivalence can be of enormous relief to the family. Furthermore, the therapist's presence as a "safe" outsider dilutes the intensity of negative feelings, making their expression a less terrifying risk.

As time goes on, the vicissitudes of anticipatory grief begin to emerge. The family often articulates what appears to be a paradox: whereas they were prepared to let go of the patient earlier in the illness, they now feel less and less able even to imagine the loss. In contrast, the patient often describes a growing accommodation—albeit painful—to the idea of impending death. This is an anguished crossroads, for it indicates the recognition that the patient and family are moving in different directions. The therapist's role is to maintain a delicate balance: facilitating the letting-go process of each person, while simultaneously creating a shared family context for the separation.

The Deepening Shade

A seven-year-old child had a recurrent dream in the year before her death: "In the dream, I want to be with my mother, and I can never quite get to her." The child recounted the dream in a joint therapy session with her mother. Whereas the mother found the dream "excruciating," her daughter stipulated that "even though the dream is very sad, it's not a nightmare." The dream which so poignantly represented attachment and loss, provided the focal image for mother and child to work through the anticipatory grief process.

With a prolonged remission, the patient or family may begin to doubt the possibility of the disease ever recurring. They may even question the accuracy of the original diagnosis. The patient, in particular, feels a sense of disjunction: bearing the diagnosis of a life-threatening illness, while looking and feeling "normal." A realistic grounding in the facts alternates continually with a longed-for hope of unlimited time. The struggle goes on within each person, as well as among family members.

I find one of the most difficult things for me is to keep my own body and psyche "in sync" so as not to be tempted to avoid treatment or to invest unrealistically in the future. This often means being "out of sync" with others around me who are convinced that I no longer need treatment since I am in a prolonged first remission. (Jaffe and Jaffe, 1977, p. 197)

This aspect of being "out of sync" is a normal and recurring theme in the anticipatory grief process. If the therapist guides the patient and family toward understanding the fluctuation, they will tolerate it without undue stress. However, when the rift between "what appears" and "what is" causes a dysfunc-

70

tional level of anxiety, active therapeutic intervention may be necessary for the family to redress the balance.

Both the patient and the family suffer from the pressure of living in the suspension of neutral time. As one patient stated: "My main problem is that I don't know whether to prepare for living or for dying." The sense of unrelenting anticipation is mitigated for the patient by the gratitude for extra time. It is the family who often express the fear that the wait will never end, that it will be interminable. They may begin to resent the patient for "still being alive," and then be flooded with enormous guilt at daring to harbor such an unacceptable thought. The family members must be given the opportunity to ventilate these feelings in sessions which do not include the patient. It is critical that the family understand that "wanting to get it over with" is a normal reaction to the stress of anticipating someone's death.

The mother of an eleven-year-old girl who had been diagnosed with leukemia at the age of three said: "I'm scared and sad about this being the final stretch ahead. But I can't take 'waiting for the other shoe to drop' much longer. As hard as her death will be, it will also be a relief. Our family needs to get on with living."

The real problem with having cancer is that people get tired of waiting for you to die of it. Perhaps I am too obstinate or just too mulish to go ahead and accommodate them.

(Ryan and Ryan, 1979, p. 351)

Ryan's statement, with its touch of irony, attests to the patient's highly tuned vigilance regarding others' impatience or discomfort. The fear of abandonment is paramount: under the prolonged stress of "waiting," will the family burn out from exhaustion, or flee? In fact, premature disengagement by the family does occur in some instances. In a self-protective move against loss and further pain, the family seems to "leave before being left." Such disengagement may be seen in a family's general emotional withdrawal from the patient, or it may take specific forms. For example, a healthy spouse may seek new attachments, or parents of an ill child may begin to focus on the sibling nearest in age to the patient. These attempts at replacement are neither inevitable, nor, when they occur, irreversible. However, they do signify a family's difficulty in negotiating a phase of the anticipatory grief process. It is crucial that the family not feel chastized for their distancing maneuvers. Instead, psychotherapy can help a family stay at, or return to, the level of thought ("I wish I could just leave all this grief behind") rather than translate the wish into action.

When the patient's illness is a cycle of remissions and relapses, the risk of family disengagement is particularly high. Both patient and family have to prepare for loss with each announcement of relapse, only to rearrange for life when remission is attained. The sense of exhaustion that accompanies this process is inordinate. The family begins to feel as if someone is "crying wolf"; it becomes increasingly difficult to know how to direct and apportion emotional energy. A similar discomfort may occur when a patient lives beyond his or her prognostic expectancy. On the one hand the family is jubilant at "beating the statistics"; more covertly however, they may wonder how to reintegrate the patient into their midst.

Anticipatory Grief

The siblings of a pediatric patient complained to the therapist: "Every holiday our parents say: 'Let's make this holiday perfect for your brother, since it may be his last.' Meanwhile, he has lived for four years. How long are we supposed to keep this up?"

A certain parallel disengagement between the patient and family is a necessary and functional part of the anticipatory grief process. However, the fine line between "disengagement" and "abandonment" separates worlds of experience. Psychotherapy functions as an integrative medium for the family who feels under threat of disintegration. The patient and family learn that the sharing of feelings can bring richness, rather than rupture, to the time which remains. They find a level of mutual investment which facilitates their adaptation to the ebb and flow of attachment and impending loss.

Of those of us diagnosed around the same time, only I am still alive. Now when I come into the hospital for treatment, I keep my door closed. I no longer want to meet other patients. It's too hard to grow close and then lose them. And too painful a reminder of my own situation. . . .

Enormous grief—and anticipatory grief—are engendered by the death of another patient. The reverberations are particularly intense when the patient who died had the same disease. On one level, the patient and family mourn the loss of a relationship. On a deeper level, the patient is struck with the awareness: "This could have been me . . . and will I be next?" This close sense of identification provides a vehicle for the patient and family to address their own sadness and fear.

73

The Deepening Shade

It is often a time for the caregiver to be actively present and reassuring, until the anxiety and grief abate.

An adolescent asked her physician: "Am I going to die from this tumor? . . . And can I ask you a personal question: are you going to cry when I die?"

In this confrontation are embedded the ramifications of anticipatory grief for the patient-caregiver relationship. Rarely do patients speak with such candor: the risk of triggering the caregiver's anxiety is too high. As the patient fears abandonment by the family, so too is he or she wary of stirring up intensity within the caregiving relationship. Furthermore, in expressing deep fears to the caregiver, the patient is all the more confronted with their reality. For these reasons, the patient often chooses to talk to those caregivers whose impact on "survival" is less than that of the physician.

The mother of an adolescent patient reflected to the therapist: "My daughter's doctor is so attached to her that I hate to bring up questions about relapse with him. I don't want him to move away from her because of his own feelings. It's wonderful that he cares so much, yet it makes it hard to bring up painful topics."

Both patient and family are careful not to express anger toward the caregiver. A woman commented with humor: "If only I knew a foreign language, I could swear at the doctors without their knowing!" The individual fears that in retaliation for expressing anger, he or she will receive a lesser quality of care; thus the source of "overly good" patient behavior. When a caregiver does distance after a patient's outburst of anger, it may be out of anxiety and bewilderment, rather than actual retaliation. In these instances, it is often the therapist who can explain the patient or family's behavior. Psychotherapy provides a context in which the individual can safely ventilate anger, conceptualize its source and meaning, and then channel it effectively. In this way, the inappropriate displacement of anger is precluded.

The physician's presence is crucial at the time of treatment decisions, particularly during a prolonged living-dying interval. The patient and family may be frightened of bearing responsibility for decisions of high-risk outcome. The family's lurking fear of somehow harming the patient, intensified by the unspoken wish to "get it all over with," is an emotionally laden situation which may require intervention. This is particularly true when parents must make critical decisions for a child who is not an active participant in the consent process. Like the therapist, the physician must be sensitive to implicit and explicit cues from the patient and family as to the extent of his or her presence and active participation.

Sometimes one memorizes a scene without knowing why, but I knew too well the reason I wanted to fix that homecoming in my mind. Even then I was beginning to store up memories against the time when there might be no others. (Ryan and Ryan, 1979, p. 108)

Anticipatory grief is a process in which the patient and family flow between a sense of relatedness and a sense of letting go. The patient, who is preparing for the loss of everything and everyone, gradually gives up the peripheral, while remaining ultimately attached to those closest.

Since there are no social rituals to mark anticipatory grief, as there are in bereavement, the process projects an aura of mystery. The patient and family may be threatened by their intense emotions, not understanding the source. Furthermore, a profound sense of loneliness accompanies the experience of anticipatory grief. Without an identity as a social phenomenon, people not directly involved are often confused as to what the patient and family are experiencing, or how to help.

The ebb and flow of anticipatory grief charts an individual course for each family, dependent to some extent on the nature and length of the illness trajectory. It is clearest at the time of diagnosis, and then must be confronted full force during the terminal phase of the illness. However, within a prolonged living-dying interval, the vicissitudes of anticipatory grief may only be evident in highly derivative form.

7

Terminal

The oncoming darkness . . .
—Theodore Roethke

"TERMINAL" IS THE LAST PHASE of the illness trajectory. Broadly defined, it refers to the time when the patient's illness no longer responds to conventional treatment. Yet the individual may still continue to live quite productively for weeks or even months, either on experimental treatment, or on no treatment at all. In a more delimited sense, "terminal" refers to the endpoint when, regardless of the status of treatment, the patient's death is imminent. In response to internal body signals, the individual begins a final withdrawal and disengagement. Inclusive of both aspects of the terminal phase, supportive care and pain control are central concerns. At a time so difficult for the patient, family, and caregiver, complex decisions must be handled. Any psychological intervention during this phase demands to be finely honed in its impact.

A critical juncture is reached when the patient no longer responds to conventional treatment. Both patient and family are usually well aware of the diminishing—or nonexistent—options. A six-year-old child provided the following explanation for the death of another patient: "The doctors ran out of medicine, and when they ran out of medicine, they lost control of his disease." Although this child may have understood the loss of options in a concrete way (as if there were no bottles of medicine left on the shelf), he nonetheless captures the nightmare experience of patients who watch life-giving options dwindle before their eyes. It is at this time that one so often hears the patient quiz the physician: "If this medicine doesn't work, then what? What will you give me next?"

The patient and family are presented with any remaining treatment options, or with a palliative care plan. This information is painful to give and receive, since there cannot be any promise for prolonged time. The essential message is that the patient has now failed to respond to conventional therapy. There are no further options whose efficacy is known. In some cases there may be an experimental treatment which, at best, might prolong survival for a brief period. The other choice is to stop treatment altogether. In all instances, the patient is assured that he or she will be kept as comfortable and as pain-free as possible.

The patient and family need time to consider whatever limited options exist. The choice between cessation versus experimental treatment usually revolves around a quality of life decision for the patient's remaining time. Thus, the patient and family ask about discomforting side effects of the experimental regimen, as well as about procedures or hospitalizations which would be necessitated by its trial. Questions then arise as to the nature of support to be provided were therapy entirely discontinued.

The patient and family base their decision on a host of factors: some are openly articulated, while others may be of a private religious or historical nature. The physician's attitude regarding the continuation of treatment also enters as an influence. Reasons for refusing further intervention include the failure of the most powerful treatment, and the suffering already endured by the patient. If the chances of forestalling death are small—and especially if the process would involve further discomfort—then the choice is to stop. The patient wants his or her time to be free from the invasiveness of treatment which bears so little promise.

For certain individuals, the thought of ending treatment is intolerable. Their message is clear: no matter how minute the chance for improvement, all options must be exercised. The patient may express distress at leaving any stone unturned. The family often states: "What if in the future we were to find out that the experimental drug does have impact on this disease and we hadn't tried it? We would not be able to live with ourselves."

There are occasions when the physician is "out of sync" with the patient and family regarding treatment options. For example, the physician may be prepared to stop treatment before the patient and family are ready. Or, "overtreating" beyond constructive limits may reflect the physician's difficulty in admitting having lost the battle with the disease. In such cases, the patient may have accepted the inevitable long before the caregiver. As a patient stated: "Look at me—I'm wasting away. Yet my doctor is still giving me the song and dance about cure." The crucial question becomes: Whose need to treat is being represented?

The process of coming to a decision can be excruciating: the sense of responsibility for oneself or for someone close is awesome. However, with its resolution, most patients and families express relief, even serenity. It is thus vital that the physician and caregiving team support the decision, even when it would not have been their option of choice.

From the time of diagnosis, pain is the essence of an individual's fear—and all too often—of his or her experience.

The Deepening Shade

The desperation is reflected in a patient's plea: "I know I'm going to die, but would you get rid of the pain? Time is short, so if anything is going to help, do it *now*." A hallmark of the hospice movement is the enlightened use of pain medication, including narcotics, during the terminal phase. The goal is to give the individual as pain-free an existence as possible, while maintaining his or her maximum alertness. Rather than treat pain "after the fact," the aim is to anticipate and prevent that pain from being experienced. By the regular administration of analgesics at the correct dose and interval, the cycle of anticipatory anxiety which overlays the physical pain is broken. In traditional settings, one often hears objections to giving narcotics, for fear that the patient will become addicted. The irony of this stance is evident and most often reflects the caregiver's inability to acknowledge a patient's terminal status.

When the patient is given the option of being at home or in the hospital, the management of pain is the critical concern. If effective pain control can be assured, the patient often chooses to remain at home. The family also needs this reassurance to assuage their terror of being helpless in the face of the patient's anguish. In other instances, the patient may choose to remain in the hospital for its secure availability of caregivers. In either setting, once pain control has been achieved, the patient is free to focus on other concerns.

I'm not going to have any hair before I die. What if I can't walk again before I die? I need my family now—all the support I can get. What will happen to them after I die?

Terminal

Embedded in these words is a woman's physical and emotional sense of her own terminality. As in all phases of the illness, the patient often possesses an inner wisdom of the body, now an awareness of the imminence of death. This palpable sense may precede medical corroboration, yet its power is undeniable.

On all of his hospital admissions, a three-year-old child played the same ritual with a stuffed duck and an ambulance: "Ducky sick; Ducky go to hospital; Ducky get better." During what turned out to be his terminal admission, the child changed the ritual: "Ducky sick; Ducky go to hospital; Ducky die."

A physician asked a man to sit up to be examined. The patient refused. Even when the physician offered her assistance, he continued to refuse, quietly and firmly. His behavior was uncharacteristic, since he had always been an extremely cooperative patient. The physician sensed that, at this time, he was declining any intervention. "It was as if he simply had no further volition to carry out any action, as if he were saying: 'This really isn't necessary. It doesn't matter anymore.'" A few days later, the man died.

Accompanying this inner sense often comes fear and desperation, the experience of being overwhelmingly out of control. The feeling of impending catastrophe is vividly illustrated in a story recounted by a dying child:

The T.V. fell off the wall and the I.V. pole crashed on the dinosaur and then the lights turned out and then the bed turned back to the wall. The door slammed, the walls fell, and the hospital broke down on the dinosaur.

The patient reaches out for reassurance, if not that death can be avoided, then that he or she will be kept comfortable and will not be abandoned. In a last effort to exert control over the inevitable, he or she may ask what to expect in these final days.

The endpoint of the terminal phase is marked by a turning inward on the part of the patient, a pulling back from the external world. The patient's sphere of concerns constricts markedly to include only the most essential and intimate: control of pain, and communincation with those closest. In fact, the patient may talk very little and may even withdraw from physical contact. A generalized irritability is also not uncommon. The individual's degree of withdrawal is contingent on many factors including: physical debilitation and pain, depression, conflict in relationships, and general style of coping throughout the illness. However, despite differences in manifestation, such inwardness is a commonality. It is the necessary and inevitable preparation for the ultimate separation of death.

The man who is really dying . . . is far more likely to think of the pain and suffering from which death is going to release him. . . . He discovers for himself the truth of the observation that it is the living who fear death, not the dying; when he says to himself: "I want to die." There is a terrible finality about those four words. They bring everything to a full stop. . . . With four words he has cut himself loose from the ordinary world and set himself apart from the majority of mankind, to whom life is still worth living and death still the ultimate horror.   (Bell, 1961, p. 241)

A six-year-old child had a wide assortment of stuffed animals, all of whom he referred to as his "sons and nephews." Whenever he was in the hospital, he kept the animals piled on his pillow. A few

84

days before he died, his mother noticed him pushing the animals away. "Don't you want your sons near you?" she asked. The child replied: "I don't have any sons anymore." These were the last words he spoke.

The family members may be hurt and perplexed by the patient's withdrawal. It is critical that they understand the behavior as a normal and expectable precursor to death: a pulling into oneself, rather than away from others. In a last burst of desperation, the family may plead with the patient not to die, expressing their dread of being abandoned. To a certain extent, the patient accepts these statements as a testimony of love and grief. However, the pleas may also evoke profound anguish, guilt, and powerlessness. In some cases, the patient may give up more quickly in order to spare the family further stress.

Therapeutic intervention can be critical in facilitating the letting go process at this ultimate point. The family must be able to give the patient implicit "permission" to die. The therapist may suggest that the patient and family say or ask anything which has remained unspoken. An adolescent's statement to her parents illustrates the power of this simple and unobtrusive intervention:

I don't want to leave you. I'm not supposed to have cancer at my age. You both took such good care of me at home. You came faster than the nurses when I called. Everyone is crying—why is everyone crying here? Something very tragic must be happening.

While such a dramatic epilogue is rarely forthcoming, the opportunity for disclosure should be made available if the patient is alert. However, under no circumstances may the therapist ever attempt to force the expression of "final words."

The patient-family synchrony of the terminal phase is different from that of other crisis points in the illness. Initially, as the end approaches, the patient and family cling together as if to ward off the onslaught of death. However, such undiluted synchrony can only be maintained if death occurs quickly. For, as the days or even weeks begin to pass, the patient's disengagement makes vivid the ultimate realization: he or she must die alone.

During the terminal phase, the family may choose to stay with the patient constantly, maintaining a vigil for whatever time remains. In other instances, particularly with a prolonged dying, the family may need to take time away, to leave. The caregiving team must support the family's way of being—or not being—with the patient, helping them to monitor their physical and emotional reserves. In order not to be burdened in critical last moments, or in the onrush of grief, the family may take care of decisions such as consent for autopsy or funeral arrangements before the patient's death. In contrast, there are families who express an almost superstitious fear of "inviting death" by making such plans ahead of time.

The family needs ongoing information about the patient's condition, with preparation for what to expect as death approaches. This final wait is excruciating for the family: there is no way out of the pain. They sense palpably what life will be like without the patient.

The theme of life-threatening illness is the interweaving of life and death forces. The terminal phase is the microcosm of this confluence.

Terminal

Death ends a life, but it does not end a relationship, which struggles on in the survivor's mind toward some resolution, which it never finds.

(Anderson, 1974, p. 77)

Such is the reality which confronts the bereaved family. All the issues with which the patient grappled—loss of control, loss of identity, and loss of relationships—now, in mirror image, become their legacy.

8

A Life of My Own

Katharine is a nineteen-year-old woman who was diagnosed as having osteogenic sarcoma at the age of sixteen. The following interview highlights the critical issues which confront the individual with a life-threatening illness. While the themes are universal, Katharine's ability to articulate complex feelings and experience is unique.

*Looking back, Katharine, what led you
to know that something was wrong?
What were the symptoms, and how
were you diagnosed?*

I was very athletic, and I was having a
lot of pain. Not frequently, but when it
happened, it was one of those pains that
wasn't normal and wasn't fun. I didn't
have any kind of bruise or swelling. It
would only hurt me when I put weight
on that leg. The pain startled me. It was
kind of my awareness of my own body.
I knew I hadn't hurt myself. I knew I
hadn't fallen. I knew it was a weird pain,
and I wanted to get it looked at right
away. So I made an appointment with
our family doctor. He just touched my
leg where it was tender and had it
X-rayed. He called a couple of days later,
and I spoke to him on the phone. He
said that it was something he could not
deal with because it wasn't his specialty.
So he sent me to an orthopedic surgeon.
It happened very fast.

*Did you suspect that it could be
anything serious?*

I did, although I don't think I ever

*wisdom of the body/
awareness of symptoms*

*preconscious awareness
of serious implications*

*patient catapulted into
pressurized time*

91

admitted to myself that I could have osteogenic sarcoma or anything like that. I knew that it had to be kind of serious because it was very mysterious. The next morning my mother took me out of school—right out of my classroom—and we went to the orthopedic surgeon. He was very nice. He said that it was either good or bad, and that he would do a bone biopsy, and that was it. But I didn't understand. I kept saying: "Wait a minute! I have to go back to school and take my test." But it was very fast. I didn't see any of my friends. I had left school at 10 A.M., was admitted to the local hospital that afternoon, and had the biopsy the next day. I think it took two days before they got the results. The doctor came in and he said: "It's not good. Go to Boston." He gave me a referral to Dr. X, an orthopedic surgeon.

emergence of conscious fear

loss of control: fear translates into actuality

Even then you were not told the diagnosis; only that it was "not good."

Well, he said that it was a bone cancer. I didn't get the technical name right away. Actually, I don't think he said "cancer"; I think he probably said "malignancy" or "tumor," but he rarely said

caregiver's difficulty in communicating "bad" diagnosis; avoidance of word "cancer"

"cancer." When he told me that I had to
go to Boston, I knew it was serious. Plus   *patient registers signals*
he said: "They will know how to take
better care of you in Boston. They have
treatments there which they can give
you." It was like: "Oh, let's not say too
much now." I kind of knew that.

You were getting a lot of signals. . . .

   When he said that it was bad and that   *attempt to assert control:*
I would have to go to Boston, I was very   *isolation of affect*
businesslike. I said: "Okay, just pack the
clothes and let's go." I really didn't have   *immediate sense of*
time. I just wanted to get it over with, to   *limits of finite time*
get done whatever I had to have done,
and not spend a lot of time. When I got
to Boston, I saw Dr. X. Then X-ray after
X-ray, hours and hours of X-rays.

How did Dr. X present the diagnosis
and what it meant? Who was with
you then?

   Almost everyone in my family was   *family presence as signal*
there—another indication that it was   *of seriousness*
bad. Dr. X came in and told me what it
was, and my options. He was very quiet.   *graphic memory of*
It's like—he knows what he has to say is   *being told diagnosis*
bad. He was very gentle. He told me
that I had osteogenic sarcoma, and that
I had two options: "You can have your

93

leg amputated, we can take the leg . . . or you can have a resection." He should have mentioned the resection first. He explained how they remove the bone and the knee joint and replace them with a metal rod. You can walk, you can keep your own leg. It looks normal. You have a long scar, but you can have as much as a 90° bend. He said that I could lead a pretty active and normal life. After he told me that, I was a little more calm.

patient as partner through shared information

What was your reaction to the word "amputation"?

I said to him, and I still say: "You're not taking the leg, in any which way, form or shape. No way." I cried, and I think I cried more because everyone else was crying around my bed. I kept saying: "I'm not having my leg removed, so just tell me more about this resection." *Everyone* was crying; it was really awful. My father was crying and he never cries. My mother was crying and saying: "I wish it were me." I hated that. I think that the family should be prepared on how to react. I don't think the person should see them that way until the person has handled it.

anticipatory grief: diagnosis and possible loss of leg

typical parental reaction of wanting to protect child

patient's sadness and grief intensified in witnessing family's reaction

94

A Life of My Own

It was hard for you to see their sadness.

It was very hard. It was very hard for me to see what I was doing to my family, through my sickness in my leg. I could just see it all.

You felt responsible for causing them pain.

And I didn't know how to comfort them. I was going to tell them it would be all right when I didn't know myself. So all I said—and I was very business-like even though I was crying—was: "We'll go home and discuss what you would do if it were you." But I had made up my mind right then and there that there was no way I would have my leg cut off.

helplessness

attempt to cope with grief of uncontrollable situation by distancing and use of second person ("you")

When I got home, I saw my one brother who hadn't been at the hospital. We cried when we saw one another, but we didn't say anything. Later my brothers and sisters discussed things with me, and they all said: "We think you should have the resection." You don't cry so much once you make your decision. You don't cry so much about having surgery; it's the result of it—not being able to do the things you like. Vanity is a strong word, but you worry

anticipatory grief: no need for words

decision as a form of mastery

loss of function

95

change in body image, self-image

about your physical appearance, how it's going to look, how people are going to react. I just couldn't envision this terribly deformed leg, and I kept thinking: "Maybe I should just have it cut off." But I always say that it's so nice to look down and see my foot and wiggle my toes. As long as I have that, I can overlook the disadvantages.

weighing of costs and benefits in coming to a decision

illness affects all aspects of identity and functioning

You once said: "The effect of this leg is on everything in my life. It's not just the scar; it's not just the leg. It's my athletic ability, my mobility."

It's not just physical things like running or skiing. You can't even *daydream* that you're running down the stairs or on the beach, because you can't do those things anymore. It's all right to daydream and get away from reality a little. But when you start to ignore a physical disability, it's hard to keep yourself in perspective. It was very awful. For a long time I was just thinking about my leg and my doctors and the pain and all the bad things, so for awhile I didn't even daydream. It affects you in so many ways. You're always haunted by it.

struggle to maintain perspective on reality and not slip into denial

overwhelming impact of illness and disability

How much during the first few weeks was your focus on losing that ability, your dreams and daydreams?

That didn't really happen until after I had the surgery. At first I had the attitude that I'll beat this and be the exception to the rule. Then after awhile, it beats on you. There aren't any rules. The first couple of weeks that I was getting chemotherapy, I really concentrated on being a good girl. I drank all my liquids. I would get sick and laugh it off. I would try and fight it.

need for mastery over assaultive treatment

being the "good patient": self-image and fear of alienating caregivers

Before having the resection I was so worried about the pain. I just didn't want to be a baby. I wanted to brace myself to know all the details: what are the muscle spasms like? Is it really bad pain? After the surgery I think I handled my pain fairly well. I recovered very fast. My doctor told me I would be hospitalized for fourteen days, and I left after nine. It was like a game: "Let's get well. Let's get away from the pain and beat the record." You have to think of it that way, because it's so easy just to lie on your bed, take your pain medicine, look at your leg and say: "Oh." But I always wanted to be home rather than in the hospital. I come from a large family and I am not used to being catered to. It took me a long time to accept the

patient's abhorrence of regression

loss of control over body (pain); mastery through preparation

active goal-setting and bargaining versus pull toward passivity

influence of patient's role and expectations in family of origin

97

nurses' care. I kept doing everything for myself. I had never had that kind of individualized attention before.

What role did your mother play in the early stage of your illness?

necessity for family's availability and support, especially at night

I don't think I would have survived if I hadn't had my mother for the first couple of months of my treatment, because I got very, very sick. My mother spent the nights at the hospital for at least the first seven or eight months of my treatment. She was always there. I

extreme dependence while "under siege"

was scared and I was frightened and I was sick and I needed my mother there so badly. There was never any question. I just thought: "My mother has to be here. I'm sick and I'm throwing up." It's a very vicious kind of sickness. It's there all the time—the dry heaves, the after-taste, the smell. So it's nice to have your mother there to nurse you. When I look

denial of dependence once crisis over

back now, I see that I needed my mother, but it could have been someone else to whom I felt particularly close. But my mother *had* to be there. It was

family's guilt and need to assuage helplessness

like an obsession with her.

Is this an issue: parents want to be there all the time, and the teenager begins to want more space?

98

A Life of My Own

I think so. I know that once I started to feel better, I didn't need my mother as much. But I didn't know how to tell her, because she needed to feel needed, and to think that I depended on her. Look what her daughter was going through; it's a very heavy guilt trip for the mother. After about six months, I began to tolerate my treatments better. I worked out a good system for myself where I was able to force myself to drink and keep it down. I was able to control it. It was then that I started to tell my mother: "You can go home." But she wouldn't.

That emerges as a conflict. . . .

Because you start to feel better. It's humiliating to have to go through the treatment, although you don't think in those terms when you're so sick. I never actually said to my mother: "I don't need you." But as I got better, I tried to show her that I could manage by myself. I wanted to handle it all on my own.

And for me, this is *my* cancer, this is *my* illness. It is not yours and don't try to make it yours. Everyone has problems. I felt very guilty because my mother was rarely home for the rest of the family. My younger sister would

patient's and family's needs "out of sync"

control over body and treatment

self-image: need to reassert autonomy

illness becomes part of one's own identity, to be coped with on one's own

patient's guilt and anxiety about family

99

role shifts within family

come home from school and have to cook dinner for them. I kept saying: "Mom, you should go home. The other kids need you. I can survive here." It was only for the last month or two of my treatments that she would go home at night. In fact, during the last few weeks, there were days she did not come into the hospital at all. Sometimes I got kind of bored, but I was so relieved that she was home.

need for autonomous relationship between patient and physician; patient's own sense of body and illness

There were times that my doctors would come in and ask: "How are you doing?" My mother would answer. *I* wanted to tell them how I felt. I couldn't say to her: "Mom, it's my body. I know what is going on." She felt so much that

identification of family with patient

it was her illness, because she had been there and seen me go through it. But other people can't know what you are going through, how you feel inside. I was very, very sick and I was very, very weak. But inside, I was fighting. I

self-image consistent despite outward change of illness

wanted to do this myself; I wanted to be on my own.

Do you think that this feeling is particularly true for adolescents?

I think so. The younger you are, the

development of independence and self-image

more dependent you are on your

mother. It's natural to want her there all the time. But once you are in high school, you want to be as independent as possible.. I was pretty secure in my own feelings, abilities, strengths and weaknesses. I knew that if I were really, really sick, I could call the nurses. Or that if I needed my mother, she would come right away.

trust in availability of caregivers and family

So with your kind of security, you didn't feel the need for constant presence. . . .

No. And whenever I would see the doctor, my mother would say: "What did he say? You're not telling me." I had no reason to lie; I just wanted it to be forgotten. I wanted to go in, do what was needed, and then go home and forget it. For me it was: "If I'm really sick, I will tell you. If I'm not feeling quite right, I'll let you know." But my parents were always bringing it up.

family anxiety

control by "containing" the illness

You once said that being sixteen was the hardest time in life to get cancer.

I still believe that. Younger children are not developed in themselves yet, in their own persons, in their own individualism. They can still be with their mother. Older people are away from

child's identity unformed; dependent

adult's life formed

101

adolescent caught in midst of identity formation process

their mother; they're detached, more adult. When you're in the middle, parents don't want to let you go. You want to be set free a little bit, but you want to be able to come back. I just felt that I

regrets at lost opportunities and options

was denied any sort of chance. I wish I could look back and see: "Would Katharine have been popular? Would Katharine have had lots of boyfriends? Would Katharine have starred on the varsity?" I look now, and would that have been what I wanted? I don't know. I never had the chance to find out. In-

illness leads to premature maturation

stead it was decided for me: "You are going to mature very fast right now. You have to make life-and-death decisions. You have to accept things that children who are young adults between the ages of thirteen and nineteen don't

bitterness at loss of developmental process

normally have to face." It's like: "Grow up right now and become what you have to become to deal with this." I never had the chance to be sweet sixteen. I never had the chance to be gay old seventeen. I had to automatically be an adult, and it was very hard.

"why me?"

When you were diagnosed, did you question why it had happened to you?

need to master status as victim

You ask that and you ask that. Then I reached a point where I said: "I'm glad

102

it's me because I can handle it." If it ever happened to someone in my family, I'd go crazy. I'm even glad that it didn't happen to one of my friends. I would hate to see somebody that I cared for go through what I was going through. I used to say that I would never wish it on my worst enemy. I didn't want my friends to know what I was going through, and even now, I don't think they have any idea whatsoever. My family knows, because they were right on the scene.

testimony to anguish of own experience

You once said that you felt as if everything were being taken away from you: your flesh, your hair, your soul, your teenage years.

loss of self through illness

It's very hard. You lose all self-pride and self-respect. You lose "self" really, because you lose so much weight. I knew I was skinny, but I must really have looked emaciated. It was all a part of what was happening to me. Looking back at photographs from then, I remember how much I hated having them taken. I never used to look in the mirror. Although you see yourself physically as you are, mentally you tell yourself: "Well, it's not that bad." You weigh seventy to eighty pounds; you're all

body image as integral part of self-image

confrontation of body changes with body image

103

bone; you don't have any hair, eyebrows, or eyelashes. I had a very nice wig, so that people would never know that I had lost my hair. But still, I always *sense of physical/* felt very exposed, very vulnerable. I *emotional exposure;* hated going places where I didn't know *stigma* anybody. I always felt that people were looking at me, wondering. I hated those kinds of confrontations. You don't really *effects of illness* care if you are living, because you're not *pervade one's life* really even living. You're so sick all the time. Even when you're not throwing up, and you don't have a headache, and your body isn't sore—even then, you don't feel healthy.

difficulty in maintaining As for soul, you don't even care. You *sense of self* say: "Just take it away. It's not doing me any good right now." You don't have any faith in yourself. You don't even *hatred of chemotherapy:* belong to yourself anymore. Your body *one side of ambivalence* is holding all those drugs, all those artificial means, and being affected so strongly by them. I hated that, and did not *need for control over* want to accept it. For the longest time, I *body* wasn't being put to sleep during treatments because I insisted on knowing what was going on. I had to see what they were doing. After awhile, because I was so sick and losing weight so rapid-

104

ly, they suggested that I go to sleep. I was surprised at how much it helped me.

For the first few months you have a very weird fascination with the treatment. You're so scared, and you think about miracle drugs. It's as if all of a sudden the drugs are going to help you, and you're going to be—I don't know "cured"—but you're going to be well. You're so gung-ho on the treatment; you're going to give it your best shot. But then it becomes: "What are they doing to me? They're putting all these needles in me with gross orange stuff going into my veins." Toward the end of my treatment I resented it so much. I didn't want any part of this disease. I just wanted to get what they were going to give me, and not have anything to do with it. I don't know if that's a common feeling: "Put me to sleep, get the medicine in, and wake me up when it's over."

I remember that at times during the year of treatment, you felt very let down and isolated by your friends.

Friends don't know how to react. It's not as if you had pneumonia and are better. You had a *cancer*, and just the

chemotherapy as lifeline: other side of ambivalence

anger at illness, treatment, caregivers emerges; too desperately sick to acknowledge it earlier

withdrawal for self-preservation

social and emotional isolation engendered by illness

people fearful and unrehearsed in dealing with life-threatening illness; stigma of cancer name "cancer" is so frightening. They don't know what you are going through. So mostly you're alone, and I think you depend very heavily on family.

family support as critical mainstay

You depend on your family, and from what you've told me, on yourself.
You once said that your teddy bear was getting your tears at night.

patient grieves alone at night

Yes, because I don't want my family to see me cry, to see what it makes me feel inside. I want them to believe that I've accepted it, which I have; that I've overlooked it, which I have; and that I am carrying on, which I am. I don't want them to know how deeply it has affected me, how regretful, cynical, whatever. It's not that they will love me any more or any less. It's just that all of a sudden they'll think that they are going to lose someone they've had all their lives. It's a very heavy load to carry on your shoulders.

patient tries to protect family from his or her pain/ overcompensation and denial

patient's grieving for self projected onto family; means of achieving distance from profound threat

Now everything is just about back to normal. One time my sister was yelling at me and she said: "Oh, you're just like you used to be before you got sick. You'd think that you would have changed." It fascinated me and I said: "Thank God I didn't change." Maybe they were all thinking or hoping in the back of their

others' almost magical expectation that patient will change in desirable ways through illness

importance of maintaining self-image as before

106

minds that I would emerge a better person.

You want to believe that you haven't changed, and that you can manage, but I was really sick. During my junior year of high school I missed over a hundred days, and I still got all A's. I kept asking myself: "Did you really get all those A's, or did they just feel sorry for you and give you the marks?" At first it bothered me, but by my senior year I said: "I'll take whatever they want to give me because I deserve it." I never asked for a break, or indicated that I wanted special favors. I just wanted to be treated normally.

need for normal role continuity

About a year after the resection, the steel rod in your leg broke. What actually happened?

I had been having pain, but I never learned and still don't know how to judge it. What's bad, what's good—I just try to endure. If it's pain that I've never had before, rather than boring pain, I'll eventually come to my senses. The pain in my leg was really bothering me, but nothing showed up on the X-ray, so I just figured it was sore.

control over body (pain)

awareness of body signals

acceptance of chronicity

One day I was sitting on the ground waiting for my ride from school. I stood up and it was like—I couldn't feel my foot. I had no idea of what had happened. Then I realized that I was not *control through mastery of medical information* attached. They cut the femur, and they cut the tibia, so there's nothing in the middle except your skin. That's literally the casing. My knee was spinning around and when I picked up the bottom of my foot, it just twirled around. There was no way that I could control *emotional panic triggered by physical loss of control* it; I was not connected at all. It was crazy. I thought that I was going to lose my leg. I was trying to be calm even though it hurt me. My parents brought me directly to Boston.

complexity of relationship with physician *At that point you felt that you had somehow failed your surgeon.*

When you've had such experimental surgery, you want to please your doctor. I had been only the twelfth or thirteenth patient to have the resection. Dr. X had *importance of physician's regard for patient's sense of self-esteem* been very proud of me. He used to display me to all the interns and say: "Look how well she is doing." I wanted to be good not just for myself, but for him, *physician as "savior"* because he had thought up the idea of the resection. I mean, he saved my leg. So when the rod broke, I really felt *self-blame: anger toward physician too threatening* awful. I kept saying: "Maybe I wasn't careful. Maybe I didn't wait long enough." But I knew that I hadn't put the leg in any danger.

After the repair surgery, you felt as if the leg wasn't really yours anymore, "that it belonged to the surgeon."

Before surgery, Dr. X had said: "This procedure will only take a couple of hours. It won't be as painful as the resection, because I'm not cutting any muscles. I'll have to chip away the old part, which is cemented to the inside of your bone, and then replace it." Unbeknownst to me, Dr. X broke the bone during the operation and had to do a bone graft, an exceedingly painful procedure. When I woke up, I was in agony, totally dazed and confused. I couldn't understand why I was in so much pain. When Dr. X explained what had happened, he made it sound as if the leg were so very fragile, as if it were made of glass. I just felt: "This isn't even my leg. This isn't my body." I bargained for a metal knee joint and a 90° bend. What I got was a leg that I can't bear weight on and a 45° bend.

Dr. X was God to me: he saved my leg and he doesn't make mistakes. But then you realize that he's only human. You can't expect him to make you an

loss of control over body

terror of the unexpected

loss: anger at unfulfilled bargain

transference issues: physician as "savior" becomes fallible human "adopted daughter" just because he saved your leg. After this second surgery, I got things into perspective. At first it had been: "Okay, Doc, anything you say." Later on, when I kept having problems, I insisted on knowing what was going on. I began to take a more active role instead of just sitting back and letting him do whatever he was going to do.

shift from passive compliance to active assertion

A few months later you had a routine chest X-ray, and they found a spot on your lung.

recurrence of the illness

There's a song that says: "What's too painful to remember, we choose to forget." When they call you back after a chest X-ray, you kind of figure that something is suspicious.

need to suppress painful memories in order to cope

patient's awareness of signals

At that time you said that having a recurrence of the disease was like alphabetical order: You know you'll be called; it's just a matter of when.

sense of fatalism

That was because two guys, good friends of mine, had already had recurrences. I was very upset when the first guy got it. The second boy had started treatment just before me. So I had this funny feeling that I was going to get it. When Dr. Y [oncologist] told me, I

network among patients

wasn't even surprised. This was another business deal as far as I was concerned. But my mother was very, very upset. I just looked at Dr. Y and said: "Well, schedule me for whatever is necessary; but if you'll excuse me, I have to go home and study for a test." There was nothing I could do about it. It was a small spot, not anything terribly serious. Anyone told that they have a spot on their lung might think they're dying; but as far as I was concerned, it wasn't spreading and I didn't want to make a big production of it. I told my family: "I don't want anyone—no one—to know about this because I don't want them worrying. Afterwards I'll tell them: 'Hey, they took it out. I'm fine.' And they can say: 'Case closed.'" But it didn't work out that way. People knew.

I had the thoracotomy right away. Once again I said: "I'll do it, I'll get it over with, and that's it." After the surgery Dr. Y suggested that I consider the option of undergoing new treatment. I was so upset. I said: "How can you ask me to do that? After my year of treatment, I told you I could never go through it again. That wasn't irrational. I made the statement under perfectly

emotional control through isolation of affect

recognition of limits of control

form of denial: minimize implications of spot

fatalistic ring of "case closed"

consistency of style of coping

anger and dread

111

normal conditions. I asked you specifically not to put me through it again." But, as a doctor, he cannot really make that promise.

quality versus quantity of life

When you first get sick, you have to live. You've got to have the years, you've got to have the time to do things, you've got to. But the second time around I said: "Now it's not the quantity of years; it's the quality of years." I had just gotten back to school and my friends. I was gaining weight and my hair had grown back. I was just getting back into a niche. And then I'm told to consider a new kind of treatment that's only been done once before. I would lose my new hair that I liked. I just said: "No. Don't ask." Now I am legally an adult. I still— no matter how bad I am—I still don't think I could go through chemotherapy again. I'd have to wait for the circumstances. But at that point, I didn't want to be denied my senior year. I didn't want to be denied so many things.

reentry process

importance of feeling in control of consent and timing

emergence of compromise in confronting reality

My parents went crazy when the spot on my lung was found, as if they were going to lose something. I kept saying: "This isn't a question of life or death, so will you stop making it sound so serious?" My mother did not want me to go for the chemotherapy. She'd been there

family's anticipatory grief versus patient's need to minimize implications

intensity of family process around treatment decision

with me and didn't want to go through it again. What I go through she goes through. My father wanted me to do the treatment. As far as he was concerned, he didn't want to lose his daughter. That's all he kept thinking: "I don't want to lose my daughter, so do it, do it, quick. Just do whatever you have to do." I mean, this is not the issue.

patient's need for distance from overwhelming threat

Was that ever an issue for you— thinking about life and death?

I think that many times I felt I had to do something or I might suffer consequences. But I don't think I ever thought that it would cause my death. You think about dying all the time because you're so sick. But I don't think I ever thought that this would be the death of me. I always seemed to be in control even though I was always sick and sometimes even toxic. I felt that since treatment had worked for other people, it should work for me. They didn't make a big production of the spot on my lung. They simply said: "We'll cut it out and hopefully we'll get it all." So I never felt threatened by it.

note process of doing and undoing: acknowledges and then denies threat of death

What role does a psychologist play for you and other patients?

You don't look at me like other people

goal of psychotherapy: enhance patient's sense of control over life

113

do and judge my behavior. Instead you analyze my behavior and try to get to the root of it. Mostly you helped *me* get to the root of it, and helped *me* handle it on my own. You can ask for your family's support, wisdom, experience; but it's not fair to burden them. I have an older sister whom I talk to, but at the same time, I don't want to upset her. I don't want to make her cry for me.

desire to protect family/ profound fear of family burnout

I know that when I first met you, I didn't want to talk about it. I wanted to handle it on my own. But that faded so quickly because you're so helpless. You really do need somebody that can come in and help you. I think it takes awhile for people. Some people who went through it never talked to the psychologists who were available. They put their faith in God or in their family circle, and they handled it on their own.

therapeutic alliance takes time to develop

importance of support systems

Is there a support network among patients?

I think so. You love them like brothers and sisters in a whole different way. You can relate to them because they know what you are going through. They can say: "Yes, I know exactly how you feel. I haven't had that pain, but I've had this one." They have all gone through the

intimacy and loyalty through shared identity

114

same humiliations, the abasement of
self. It's like people who come back from
war. They have a kind of togetherness
that you can only feel if you've been
through the same experience. I always
want to know how the other kids are
doing, and I try to keep in touch. There
were times that I didn't want to see
them. I knew that they knew what I was
feeling, and I hated it. Or if I were really
sick, I didn't want them to know. Sometimes they served as a reminder, and I
didn't want to know or talk to them just
then. But those phases are few and far
between and don't last long.

facing other patients allows no escape from oneself

protectiveness

You still want the chance to have
"normal" friends who have never experienced being sick. You don't want to
be denied those friends either. You don't
want to become a clique with people
based on illness. That would be kind of
weird.

identity as patient must not become total identity

*One of your friends to whom you were
close from the beginning just died.
What do you feel when someone with
the same illness dies?*

I'm sure some people are frightened
by it. I'm sure sometimes they're scared.
. . . It breaks your heart more than you
think. You want everyone to make it.

need for distance from pain: use of second and third person ("you" and "they")

115

You want everybody to experience any type of good time that you have. You know how frustrating it is to be denied it. I know that I thought several times that I wished I could have had the surgery instead of my friend. But that's the same kind of feeling that I get angry with my family for feeling. I always tried to show him that I cared. Not just because he had the sickness I had; not just because he lost his leg and I kept mine; but just because I liked him. I know I always told him that I admired him. He helped me a lot. But I don't think I ever told him that I wished it were me, because I know he would have said: "Thank God it was me and not you." I think he is better off. I don't think the world is so great today. I'm not saying that death is any better; but again, it's quality, not quantity. As I've looked, I don't think that quality means to die happy and to live sad.

close identification

appreciation of relationship beyond patient role/ profound loyalty

patient's recognition of owning and coping with one's illness

search for meaning in tragic death

You wrote a poem about the issue of quality of life.

I'm a writer, and I write a lot. But I didn't write much while I was ill. It wasn't that I wanted to give it up; I just felt that the writing would be too ugly or too awful. The last assignment in my

terror of confronting raw emotion

116

creative writing class was to describe the
event that most affected you during your
high school years. For me it was easy. It
was getting cancer and having problems
with my leg. I didn't want to write about
that and have people feel sorry for me.
How poetic can you make cancer
sound? It's just so awful. So I used a
metaphor. Without even thinking about
it, I just wrote down a comparison that
I use all the time. It describes a lot of
what I've felt, and I'm sure that other
kids would identify with it. The poem
doesn't have a title:

> They say the fox will gnaw off his
>   own limb to save his life if
>   he gets caught in a trap,
> but I have yet to see a three-legged
>   fox lazily browsing through an
>   apple orchard in late fall.
> If his need for survival so greatly
>   exceeds his sense to maintain
>   the quality of his life, I
>   hail the fox.
> I could not make such a sacrifice as he.
> He will never run at full speed through
>   the yawning fields of the countryside
>   again.
> Every time I see a fox so beautiful
>   and free,
> I wonder how the chains of man's

insensitivity can bind him
so snugly
that he forgets what it is to be
a fox.
And I feel sorry that the fox has
to make such a decision for
reasons, like mine,
which are beyond our control.

control as pivotal issue in life-threatening illness

The poem just about sums up this experience: something beyond my control. It's like the fox who runs around and gets into a trap. What does he have to say about it? Nothing. He can't sit around asking why it's he. He must make the choice: either I cut my leg off or I die. I've heard that if foxes are physically able and not weakened, they will cut off their leg. You can't lose perspective on what you are. The way I look at it, your leg is part of your body. That's how I was brought into this world, that's what it is to be me—to have both of my legs. If I had had my leg cut off without thinking, or without any choice, I know that I would have changed totally. But since I did have the option, I couldn't have it cut off. So you have to control what controls you to a certain extent. You know, your independence, your

118

self-respect: these are within your own
control.

*What has it been like for you to conjure
up memories of these past two years?*

It's not so bad. I don't mind doing it
at all. I feel that if I can help someone, I
would help in any way I can. I want to
ease people's suffering. If I can't do it
directly, I'll do it indirectly. It's such an
individualized experience which people
handle in many different ways. The way
I deal with it is to remember that I have
a life of my own.

*self-worth in making
one's own experience
meaningful for others*

119

Epilogue

WHAT ENABLES A THERAPIST to sustain quality involvement with individuals confronting life-threatening illness? How does one continue to encounter people whose lives are stripped to the essence?

The therapist must engage in an ongoing, honest appraisal of his or her capacity for repeated cycles of attachment and loss. An awareness of and respect for one's limitations is an integral part of such an assessment. It is only within the context of one's own psychic reality that the ability to take emotional risks, to experience and witness deep feelings, has meaning. Emotional risk-taking without recognition of these limits leads to an intensity which burns itself out.

The therapist's own loss history has significant impact on his or her present work with the individual confronting death. Unresolved losses loom large in such encounters. The individual in a life-threatening situation has an acute sense of vision through which the therapist's difficulties become transparent. There is little place to hide, for work with these individuals demands the therapist's use of self to an extraordinary degree. Thus, introspection must be the therapist's constant companion, with the attendant willingness to acknowledge one's own vulnerability. A basic principle in working with these families is knowing how to enter their circle, while at the same time preserving one's own boundaries.

Although no psychotherapy is ever complete, this fact is strikingly evident in work with an individual with a life-threatening illness. The therapeutic process and the illness reality are inextricably bound: interruption or termination may occur at any point. Thus, each encounter should be complete in and of itself. The therapist must possess a high tolerance for ambiguity in order to step into the lives of those whose existence is predicated on such uncertainty. He or she must have the inner freedom to flow with their experience and not need to impose a rigid structure.

The therapist can judge whether involvement with boundaries has been achieved when in response to the question: "Whose needs are being served?" the answer is unequivocal: "The patient's." An overly intense involvement often means that, for whatever reason, the therapist is living through the patient. It is thus crucial that the therapist keep his or her work in balanced perspective.

In essence, the therapist must be committed to the individual's quality of life—for however long that life may last. Furthermore, in the absence created by the patient's death, he or she can provide a sense of continuity for the family. The therapist must find meaning in a personal belief system as an antidote to the pain of investment and loss. In the words of Saint-Exupéry's Little Prince: "One runs the risk of weeping a little, if one lets himself be tamed." As time is the pivot of all therapeutic interventions, commitment emerges as the focal characteristic of the therapist. The richness and depth of this commitment are intensified by the omnipresence of separation and loss.

REFERENCES

References

Aldrich, C. K. (1974). "Some Dynamics of Anticipatory Grief." In B. Schoenberg, A. Carr, A. Kutscher, D. Peretz, and I. Goldberg (eds.), *Anticipatory Grief*. New York: Columbia University Press.

Alsop, S. (1973). *Stay of Execution*. Philadelphia: J. B. Lippincott.

Anderson, R. (1974). "Notes of a Survivor." In S. B. Troup and W. A. Greene (eds.), *The Patient, Death and the Family*. New York: Scribner.

Bell, T. (1961). *In the Midst of Life*. New York: Atheneum.

Bergler, E., and G. Roheim (1946). "Psychology of Time Perception." *Psychoanalytic Quarterly* 26: 190.

Bowen, M. (1976). "Family Reaction to Death." In P. J. Guerin, Jr. (ed.), *Family Therapy*. New York: Gardner.

Bresloff, J., M. Bresloff, and C. Goodyear (1975). "Planting Things I Won't See Flower." Videotape, United Methodist Communications.

Geist, R. (1977). "Consultation on a Pediatric Surgical Ward: Creating an Empathic Climate." *American Journal of Orthopsychiatry* 47: 432–44.

Jaffe, L. (1975). "Terminal." *Pittsburgh,* April 1975, pp. 37–40.

———, A. Jaffe, and R. Love (1976). "Living with Dying." Videotape, Alfred University School of Health Related Professions.

———, and A. Jaffe (1977). "Terminal Candor and the Coda Syndrome: A Tandem View of Fatal Illness." In H. Feifel (ed.), *New Meanings of Death*. New York: McGraw-Hill.

———, A. H. Kutscher, and L. G. Kutscher, eds. (1978). *Dialogues: The Dying and the Living*. New York: Arno Press.

Mann, J. (1973). *Time-Limited Psychotherapy*. Cambridge, Mass.: Harvard University Press.

Rappaport, S. (1980). "Our Battle with Leukemia." *Parents,* March 1980, pp. 106–14.

Roethke, T. (1975). *The Collected Poems*. Garden City, N.Y.: Doubleday.

——— (1980). *Straw for the Fire*. Seattle: University of Washington Press.

Ryan, C., and K. M. Ryan (1979). *A Private Battle*. New York: Simon and Schuster.

Saint-Exupéry, A. de (1971). *The Little Prince*. New York: Harcourt, Brace, and World.

References

Sourkes, B. (1976). Personal communication to Lois Silverstein Jaffe, 12 Jan. 1976.

——— (1977) "Facilitating Family Coping with Childhood Cancer." *Journal of Pediatric Psychology* 2, no. 2: 65–67.

——— (1980). "Siblings of the Pediatric Cancer Patient." In J. Kellerman (ed.), *Psychological Aspects of Childhood Cancer*. Springfield, Ill.: Charles C. Thomas.

CONTEMPORARY COMMUNITY HEALTH SERIES

A Mind That Found Itself
Clifford W. Beers

The Psychiatric Halfway House: A Handbook of Theory and Practice
Richard D. Budson

Racism and Mental Health: Essays
Charles V. Willie, Bernard M. Kramer, and Bertram S. Brown, Editors

Social Skills and Mental Health
Peter Trower, Bridget Bryant, and Michael Argyle

The Sociology of Physical Disability and Rehabilitation
Gary L. Albrecht, Editor

The Style and Management of a Pediatric Practice
Lee W. Bass and Jerome H. Wolfson

In cooperation with the Institute on Human Values in Medicine:

Medicine and Religion: Strategies of Care
Donald W. Shriver, Editor

Nourishing the Humanistic in Medicine: Interact ons with the Social Sciences
William R. Rogers and David Barnard, Editors